Contents

Chapter 5 Types of funding

Chapter 6 Sources of funding

This book is dedicated to all the people and organizations who have funded me and my businesses, directly or indirectly, over the years. Thank you for believing in me and my ideas, and supporting me through the early stages and into profitability.

In particular:

My parents, Roger and Sarah, and my girlfriend Anna.

Business angels: Jonathan Elvidge, Steve McDermott, E. R. Charles Lewis, Robert McKay, Julian Horrocks and John Barnes. Thanks also to HM Revenue and Customs for providing the Enterprise Investment Scheme.

Banks: HSBC, the Royal Bank of Scotland; and thanks to the DTI for providing the Small Firms Loan Guarantee Scheme.

Corporate partners: Rachael Stock and Richard Stagg at Pearson Education who put together the deals between one of my companies and theirs, and who were flexible to improve the cash flow of the deal.

Suppliers: All the suppliers to my companies who were prepared to give extended payment terms to help me get businesses up and running in the early days, and at key stages of turnaround and growth.

Customers: All the customers of my companies who agreed to make a deposit or payment in advance to help cash flow at key stages of growth in some of my businesses.

Between all of these, and a few I can't mention because they relate to my work with other people's businesses, I've used nearly every source of funding there is!

Introduction

One of the biggest challenges that entrepreneurs face in starting, running and expanding their businesses is finding the funding first to get off the ground and then to ensure that the company always has the funds in place to meet its obligations and invest in the future.

This isn't just a challenge faced by those starting companies or whose companies are in trouble. Fast-growing, successful businesses are actually as likely to have cash flow problems – and therefore financing requirements – as businesses that are struggling for sales.

This is because money is the fuel that powers your business. This means:

1. If your engine is poorly maintained it will burn fuel more quickly without getting further, or fuel may simply leak out.

2. If you're accelerating fast, it's going to burn fuel more quickly.

3. If you run out of fuel before finding somewhere to fill up, you'll be stranded and won't get to your destination.

The good news is that there is actually plenty of fuel available. I regularly hear financiers (such as business angels, bankers or venture capitalists) complaining that there is a shortage of good businesses in which to invest their money.

The key thing to note is that there is no shortage of *businesses* wanting investment – just a shortage of *good* businesses. So before we jump straight into the subject of where to find the money and how to pitch for it, we're going to spend some time having a good hard look at your company to get it into shape, ready to apply for funding.

Here's the journey we'll take in this book:

- We'll begin by taking an overview of the fundraising process, and key facts about the different types of funding.

- Then we'll look in depth and consider what investors want.

- Next we'll get your business into shape to meet these requirements.

- Once you're satisfied that your business is ready we'll consider how to prepare and present your business plan.

- Then we'll look at the types and sources of funding that are available to you, explaining how they work, what's expected of you, how expensive each type is, and how suitable each type is for different stages of your business from start-up to growth.

- Next we'll help you select the funding that is best suited for your purposes.

- After this it will be time to learn how to pitch your business to the funders, and then what to do if your application is rejected.

- Finally we'll look at how to negotiate the deal once you have the funders hooked.

This won't be an easy journey: you'll be presented with tough decisions to make, a variety of choices that will be key to the long-term development of your business, and you'll have a lot of hard work to do. But if you do follow this advice your business will be much better prepared, better funded and better placed for future success.

TERMS IN THIS BOOK

Entrepreneur. This is you. I realize you may be the finance director of a business or another member of the key team, but it's going to be a lot simpler if we stick to this one term.

Funder. This is someone who could provide finance for your business, although this could be through a variety of means. They may be an equity investor, a lender, asset financier, customer, etc., but we're going to refer to them all as funders to keep things simple.

THE WEBSITE

There is a website to support this book at **www.flyingstartups.com/ funding**. It's part of the leading online community for entrepreneurs called Flying Startups. The site provides a great chance for entrepreneurs to network, sharing advice and experience as well as contacts. It's also a chance to ask any questions you may have. I'm a very regular visitor to the site and I look forward to meeting you there!

PERFECT PARTNERS

This book is best used in combination with my other books for entrepreneurs, as well as a great business plan book by Richard Stutely:

Start Your Business Week by Week

This guide takes you through each step of launching your new business over a six-month period – from helping you find or refine an idea, to developing the business plan, finding customers and opening for business. Each week includes a to-do list, detail about the work to be done, advice from real entrepreneurs and useful contacts.

The Small Business Handbook

Designed for start-ups and established business, this book gives you an overview of everything you need to know in order to manage and expand your company, comply with regulations, improve your sales, increase your profits, satisfy customers and recruit and retain the best staff. You can read it all the way through and use the ideas and tools provided, then keep it as a desk reference to dip into as you need advice.

How to be an Entrepreneur

Being successful in your own business is more about 'soft' skills – such as managing yourself, managing other people, motivating people, attracting customers, being focused and creating opportunities – than about 'hard' technical skills such as financial expertise. This book examines the experiences and attitudes of a wide range of successful entrepreneurs to reveal exactly what the key skills and beliefs are, and how you can develop them.

The Definitive Business Plan by Richard Stutely

I didn't write this book, but have found it extremely useful, and consequently recommend it to you. In *How to Fund Your Business* we will look at the whole range of things you need to do in the process of raising funding, and the business plan is only one part of that, so we can only cover the basics. *The Definitive Business Plan* is a much more in-depth guide and you will derive considerable benefit from using the two books together.

JARGON BUSTER

Finally, if you come across any terms in this book that you don't know, they are explained near their first mention in the book, in boxes marked 'Jargon buster'. In these, I wrestle with financial terms to explain them in plain English that even your granny would understand (of course, your granny may have been an international financier before retirement, in which case you should think of somebody else's granny here).

1

CHAPTER ONE
An overview

Before we get down to the real nuts and bolts of acquiring the cash to build your business, let's take a moment to establish some key terms that will be used, and get an overview of the whole process.

STAGES OF FUNDING NEED

Throughout this book certain key stages of a company's development will be referred to. Here is an explanation of what is meant by each stage.

Seed

At this stage you have identified an opportunity, assembled your core team (which may just be you!), and perhaps some of the resources you need. Further research is still needed into opportunities and customers, and to develop your products or services. There probably hasn't been any funding provided for the business, except perhaps you covering some expenses, and you are probably doing it in your spare time.

Start-up

At this point you are ready with a product or service that can be offered to customers. You have a good idea of the kind of customers you are targeting, what they want and how to sell to them. You may even have made a few sales (which is great news!), and you may well have received some funding for the company from the management team (including yourself), friends, family and possibly a few other sources. You may still be part-time in the business, keeping a normal job to pay the bills. At this stage it is still likely to be just the founders working in the business, perhaps with a few friends or family members helping out when they can.

Early stage

You have a track record of sales, and good customer testimonials to show that your products and services are well received. By now you will most likely be working in the business full-time, and you may well have taken on some employees. The business has probably received funding from the founders, family, friends, a business angel, a bank or a grant provider. You are managing all right, but are probably not profitable yet, and growth is restricted by your limited resources. You may have had one or two setbacks to your plans and are always short of cash. Now that you have proven the opportunity, you need to raise funds to advance the company to profitability, stabilize it and perhaps take the first stages of growth. This may involve recruiting one or two key employees, investing in some equipment, premises and other resources, and some marketing.

Growth

You have been running the business for a few years and have established a successful, profitable business. You have the management team, key staff and resources you need, and you have a track record of happy customers, good service and growing sales. You could happily continue trading like this and have a comfortable lifestyle, but you have ambition. You see the opportunity to really expand the business. Perhaps you want to create a chain of shops instead of just a few, perhaps you want to start exporting your products, maybe you want to sell franchises to run your business, maybe you want to expand to other regions of the UK, or perhaps you just simply need to grow in order to cope with customer demand. You might even be considering buying another company as part of your expansion plans.

You might have received some funding from banks or business angels already, plus original investments from founders, friends and family.

Turnaround

This category is for businesses that have hit problems, which happens to most companies at some time or another. Perhaps a major customer goes bust or simply doesn't pay, or maybe a major order is delayed, it's taking longer to reach the right level of sales, or any one of a number of other problems.

Problems like these can occur at any stage of your business's growth, but the solution is the same – you need to conserve your cash carefully, and probably raise new funds to fuel the business. Unless you have been clever and watching the numbers carefully, you have probably only spotted the problem when it's too late (as most people do), so it's likely that you need to raise the cash very quickly.

It is possible to turn your business around – many, many entrepreneurs have done it. I lost count of the number of crises in some of my companies in their early stages – but (touch wood) I've never lost one yet! We always managed to identify the problem (albeit sometimes at the very last minute), tighten up on cash controls and raise new cash, while solving the problem, although sometimes it was a very tight squeeze.

However, these are the times when you learn the most important things about running a business. I learned more in the times I was solving crises than I did in any of the good times. It was an intensive education, and one that now means I have enough knowledge about fundraising to write a book on it! The things I learned in these times have also enabled me to create a much better business than had it all been plain sailing. Thus the most important thing in a turnaround situation is not to give up – there will be a lot of hard work and stress, but there is always light at the end of the tunnel. You can turn your business around, and you and the company will end up being stronger and healthier as a result.

TYPES OF FUNDING

We will look at all of the types of funding in more detail later, but it's important to understand the options and what they mean before we go any further, so here is a brief overview of the key ways to raise funds for your business.

Sales

This is the very best, but most often overlooked, way to raise cash.

Before you begin looking for any other funding it is really worth taking the time to see how you can improve the flow of cash into the business from your customers. This can be done by:

- making more sales;

- increasing your prices;

- taking payment, or part-payment, in advance;

- up-selling customers to higher value, or extra, products or services.

Special advice Seed or start-up

You can generate cash to provide the funds to develop your main business opportunity by selling something else initially that doesn't require lots of resources.

Special advice Early stage, growth or turnaround

Another option for you is to use the invoices that you have sent to customers to raise funds for your business through a system called 'invoice finance'. There are two forms of invoice finance. In the first, 'invoice discounting', the finance company advances you up to 85 per cent of the total value within about 24 hours of the invoice being generated. When the customer pays, they pay the rest of the money minus their fees and interest.

The next step up is called 'factoring', which means the finance company will also take on the work of chasing your customers for payment – fully managing your credit control procedure.

Invoice finance is like an overdraft, but linked directly to the money you are owed by your customers. Because of this security, the interest costs are lower than with an overdraft.

Many companies find that using invoice finance greatly improves their cash flow. This is a kind of asset finance (with your sales ledger being the asset in question). See p. 9 for details of asset finance.

Equity

Equity finance involves selling shares in your company to raise funds. You don't have to repay the money invested as you do with a loan, but the investor expects the value of their shares to increase over time, and eventually to be able to sell their shares for much more than they bought them for. They may also expect to be paid a percentage of the company's profits each year (this is called a 'dividend').

Jargon buster · Dividend

From time to time (usually either quarterly, half-yearly or most commonly annually), the board of directors of a company can declare a dividend. This is a payment to the shareholders out of the profits the company has made. It is usually expressed as a percentage of the profit for the period. There is no requirement to declare a dividend, unless you have a specific agreement with an investor.

Dividends are paid equally on each share of the same class of share. (More details on different classes of shares in Chapter 8.)

For example, Jingle-Jangle Ltd makes a profit of £10,000. There are two investors in the company, both holding the same class of ordinary shares. Fred owns 75 shares in the company, while Sid owns 25. They decide to declare a dividend of 10 per cent, meaning that the total to be paid to shareholders is £1000, with the rest of the profit being retained in the company to fund its growth. This means that £10 will be paid per share. So Fred receives £750 while Sid receives £250.

Dividends are a tax efficient way for investors to take money out of the company. However, many entrepreneurial companies won't declare dividends in their early years, preferring instead to keep the money in the company to fund growth.

With equity investments the investor is sharing the risk with the entrepreneur. If it all goes wrong they could lose all the money they invested. As a result they expect a much higher return on their investment if things go well.

Only standard limited companies have shares to sell, so you can't raise funds in this way for a business that has the legal status of Sole Trader, Partnership or Company Limited by Guarantee.

Equity investments usually involve the management team, friends, family, contacts, business angels or venture capitalists.

Jargon buster   Business angel

This is a wealthy individual with business experience who invests in entrepreneurial companies as part of a broader investment strategy. Business angels use their experience to spot companies that can generate high returns on their investment. As well as investing money by buying shares, they can often bring valuable contacts and knowledge to the business. If you've seen the television programme *Dragons' Den* then you can think of the 'Dragons' as business angels.

Jargon buster   Venture Capitalist

A venture capital firm manages 'funds' of money on behalf of major investors such as insurance companies, pension funds, other financial institutions and some very wealthy individuals.
Their job is to use their specialist knowledge to invest the funds in higher risk, but higher reward, companies – therefore generating higher returns in turn for the original investors without the hassle of dealing with lots of small companies. The risks are reduced by each fund investing in a wide selection of small companies with the expectation that one or two will do really well, the majority will chug along, and a few will fail.

Venture capitalists generally invest for periods of between 3 and 7 years.

Debt finance

Although this is the form of finance that most entrepreneurs turn to first, it's not always the best because of the costs. The most common forms of debt finance are loans and overdrafts, and most business owners head straight to their high street bank to apply for these, even though there are many providers out there whose rates are more competitive.

You will have to make repayments on loans, usually monthly over an agreed period, and you will also pay interest. Overdrafts attract higher interest charges, and are really only suitable for occasional, short-term use. Banks are getting stricter about offering overdrafts since a court case resulted in restrictions on the forms of security that can be taken out against overdrafts. The other potential issue with overdrafts is that they are repayable on demand – so if your bank gets nervous you might suddenly have to repay the full amount.

Credit cards are available for businesses and operate in a similar way to consumer credit cards. 'Charge cards' are also available, and these require the full balance to be paid off each month. Using these cards for making purchases can improve your cash flow, often meaning that you don't actually have to pay cash for goods until pretty much the same time that your customer pays you for the work.

You can also get debt finance from your suppliers, by applying for a trade credit account. This means that you get an agreed period after receiving the goods until you have to pay. This might be 30 days, 60 days or some other period the supplier specifies and can have a significant positive effect on your cash flow. This is a great source of funding if it's available.

Special advice Seed, start-up or early stage

In these stages of the development of your business it is best to avoid burdening the company with debt if at all possible. Do whatever you can to generate cash from sales, or by begging and borrowing whatever you need instead of paying the full rate. If you can get trade credit this can be a good form of funding, but many suppliers are reluctant to extend credit to new customers who have little or no trading history.

►

Seed-stage companies may find it difficult to raise any debt finance at all from the banks, and you may need to borrow money in a personal capacity or from friends and family to get started.

Start-up and early stage companies should be able to borrow if you have security to offer. If you can't provide security, you may be able to take advantage of the Small Firms Loan Guarantee Scheme in which the government provides the bank with the security it needs in order to give you a loan. More on this in Chapter 8.

Special advice Growth

Debt can be a very effective way to fund a growth company, as long as you can fund the repayment and interest easily. It's often used to match equity investment. So if you are raising £1m from equity investors you should be able to get a debt finance package of a similar value.

Special advice Turnaround

In this business stage you may not have much choice – the company may already have a lot of debt. If so, you should try to negotiate with the lenders or creditors to improve the terms, delay the repayments, extend the repayment period, or anything else that can improve your cash flow. It may cost you more in the long run, with higher interest, but at this stage you are far more concerned about the short term.

If possible, avoid taking on more debt, and look for equity finance or preferably funds from improved sales via one of the options listed above, or by selling some of the company's assets. You should also reduce expenditure wherever possible – most companies develop 'fat' in their budgets over time. Be brutal in cutting it all out.

If you do need to use debt finance, try first to get improved trade credit terms. Your suppliers may be willing to help you out if you have been a good customer for them, but many will be cautious if there have been signs that your business is in trouble.

Sometimes, however, you will have little choice but to fall back on a loan or overdraft, in which case make sure you can afford it even if things get a bit tighter, and make sure you shop around for the best deal. If the need is genuinely short term an overdraft will be all right, but a loan will be cheaper for long-term borrowing. Do take advice from your accountant.

Asset finance

This form of finance funds the purchase of a specific asset, and is usually secured on that asset. Sometimes it can be obtained on an asset you already own, and is again secured on that asset. Think of this as being like the mortgage on your house, but instead of your house the asset is the company van, a piece of machinery or other valuable items.

Different types of asset finance are available for different types of asset, and include:

- Commercial mortgage, which is secured on any business premises you own, and can be used to buy the premises or raise funds for other purposes if you already own them.

- Leasing or hire purchase, to purchase vehicles, machinery or other items. There are a few different forms of lease arrangement, which will be discussed later in this book.

- Hire, like hiring a car, in which you pay a fee to use a certain asset for a certain period of time, and then return it.

- Invoice finance, which we looked at in 'Sales', above (see p. 4). This raises money secured on your sales ledger.

Special advice Seed or start-up

It can be difficult to get asset finance until you have a financial track record, but you should be able to hire assets.

Initially it is best to beg and borrow any assets you need. Get a friend to let you use a desk in a corner of their office, or use your Dad's garage as a workshop. Perhaps you could buy the machinery or computers you need secondhand? Do whatever you can to get everything you need cheaply.

Special advice Turnaround

Asset finance can be a great way to release cash back into your business that has been locked up in lumps of machinery or property. You can sell these assets to a finance company for cash, and then lease them back over a fixed period. Ask your accountant or a corporate finance specialist for advice on this.

Business support

Government agencies (often operating through Business Links) and other non-profit organizations (such as charities) offer a range of financial support for businesses.

These include:

- **Grants:** You will receive a sum of money that you don't have to repay in return for creating jobs, training staff, expanding your business or undertaking other activities the government is keen to encourage such as launching a website or installing new technology.

- **Soft loans:** You are provided with a loan with very favourable repayment terms and interest.

- **Incubator programmes:** You will be provided with a place to work, some business advice and possibly some funding. You may have to give shares in return.

We will look at all these types of funding, and the sources you can obtain them from, later in the book.

In most cases it is best to raise finance from a number of sources to create the perfect mix for your situation. Most people just consider one at a time – such as rushing out to get a bank loan – but it really is best to blend them. You may be able to get a grant, but perhaps it will only cover 30 per cent of the project costs. You could then raise some equity finance with matching debt finance to cover most of the rest, and then lease some machinery you needed instead of buying it; and raising funds from sales should always be in your funding mix. Get customers to buy more, at higher prices and pay in advance – that's the mark of a true entrepreneur!

THE PROCESS OF RAISING FUNDING

How long do you expect the process of raising money for you business to take? It's a pretty safe rule that you should at least double whatever period you first think of to arrive at a realistic time-scale! Fundraising is a fairly time-consuming process, involving a lot of thought and planning – followed by a lot of meetings and negotiations. If you're raising simple debt finance for a bank (for an amount under £250k) you can expect the process to take anywhere between four weeks and four months. If you're pitching for funding from venture capitalists then it could take at least six months to a year. If you plan to raise funding by listing on public markets you should allow one to two years!

For all types of funding the process will look roughly like this:

1. Identify that your business is going to need more funding to start, grow or survive.

2. Look at what shape the business is in now. Is it ready for funding? Can you improve the business prior to raising funds in order to get a better deal?

3. Begin the planning process by working out your 'story'. What are you going to do in your business in the next few years? Which customers will you work for? What resources will you need? What funding will you need? This will all be developed into the 'words' part of your business plan.

4. Put together financial forecasts based on your 'story'. Start with a sales forecast, then add in a forecast of expenditure to get a profit and loss forecast. Then develop a cash flow forecast. This will show what funding you are going to need to raise. You now have a completed business plan.

5. Seek advice from professional advisers – accountants or corporate finance specialists. This is particularly important when you are raising larger amounts.

6. Explore potential sources of finance and put together a plan for an ideal package – probably a mix of a few different types and sources of funding.

7. Begin approaching funders to introduce your business and your plans. Send a copy of your business plan to people who are interested.

8. Hold first meetings with funders. You might make a presentation and they will have a lot of tough questions.

9. Provide any further information that may be required. For large investments the funder may carry out due diligence (see p. 31).

10. Answer any more questions that arise and provide further information.

11. Negotiate a deal with any funders who decide to provide finance.

12. Draw up agreements and other necessary paperwork.

13. Handle any last minute changes, renegotiations, etc.

14. Sign the deal!

Jargon buster **Due diligence**

This is a process of researching and confirming all the key points you made in your business plan, plus checking that nothing is wrong with the business.

This is the process for a fairly average deal. While not all of this is required if you're only raising a small amount of funding, larger amounts will require even more work. As you can see, there's going to be a lot to do – but this book will make things much more straightforward.

THE PROSPECTS FOR FUNDRAISING SUCCESS

Ironically it is much easier to raise large sums of money than small sums. This is partly because the deal will merit bringing in corporate finance specialists to assist you, but also because there is a lot of funding out there for companies with a proven track record and a good story.

The next easiest goal is to raise amounts under about £25k for start-ups, which can usually be raised from friends, family, contacts and bank debt. It's the entrepreneurs who want to raise amounts between £25k and £1m who have the most work ahead of them. I'm sorry to break the news if this includes you, but you're going to have to put in a lot of time and effort – and ensure that your business plan really gives an impressive and exciting picture of your company. You will have to be patient and professional and allow a lot of time to raise the necessary funds.

2

CHAPTER TWO

What do funders want?

Now that you have an outline understanding of the different types of funding available we can look at what funders will want from your business in exchange for their money.

Whatever type of finance the funder in question offers, they work through two stages:

1. Looking at your business. They will check that your business is suitable for investment, with a good team, a good opportunity, proper controls and good prospects.

2. Looking at the 'deal'. They will ensure that the terms of investment are suitable, giving them security and a good return.

WHAT FUNDERS LOOK FOR IN YOUR BUSINESS

Talent

Let's start by dispelling a common myth:

The business idea is the most important thing to investors.

This is simply not true. The most important consideration in any potential investment is the talent: the entrepreneur, and in larger businesses their management team, who will be running the business. It is accepted wisdom that a talented management team can make a great business out of a simple, unexciting idea, but that a bad management team can make a mess of even the most brilliant idea. Investors will be looking to see that you, and your management team, have the following:

1. **Relevant experience**. The fact is that having experience in your industry greatly increases your chance of success. Many of the most successful businesses are started by managers from large companies leaving to start a business in the same sector, or a closely related sector. They know how the industry works, who the key customers are, who the key suppliers are and what the critical success factors are. They have been schooled in the industry over many years. Funding for people like this is readily available. But although experience in your industry does make obtaining funding easier, it doesn't mean you should give up if you don't have any experience in the industry. Every now and then an outsider comes in to shake up an industry by doing things in a way that nobody else thought of, because everyone else simply focused on the 'standard' way of doing things. An outsider who doesn't know that something is supposed to be impossible can often surprise everybody by proving that it is possible.

2. **Key skills that will be useful to the business**. At the top of this list is sales. If you have proven sales skills within your team then funders will relax a little more. Funders will also often want to see either that a member of your team has solid financial experience, or that you have recruited an outside expert or member of staff to help you in this area. Slightly further down the wish-list are skills in your chosen specialism, but these aren't absolutely essential as they can be learned. I know two men who decided to set up a brewery, and although they had never brewed beer in their lives, they did have experience of the leisure industry and how the supply chain and the marketing worked. They recruited people who knew how to brew beer. It's important to note that your management team needs to have skills relevant to running that kind of business, rather than actually doing the work itself – you will be employing other people to do the actual work.

3. **Key contacts that will be useful to the business**. These may come through your experience in the industry, through your existing contacts network, or be generated through your preparation for the funding pitches because you know that funders will be looking for good contacts. Get out there and network. Read the industry newsletters, websites, etc. Go to industry events. Meet people, find

out about them. Get to know the key players in your target industry. Keep in touch with them, help them by putting them in touch with other people you meet. Can you solve any problems they have? This is how great contacts are made, not by simply looking for what they can do for you.

You need contacts for suppliers, distributors, customers, industry press, key industry figures and so on, but great contacts don't simply have to be in your target industry. They could be influential figures from the local business community, politicians, journalists, financiers and so on.

4. **An understanding of the challenges faced by the business.** No business is without challenges. Funders know this, and so should you. They will worry if you try to pretend that there are no challenges on the horizon, so it is important to analyze carefully the challenges you will face. What will be difficult about creating or expanding your supply chain and running it effectively? What will be difficult about persuading customers to buy? What will be difficult about running the business internally? What other problems could occur? Is your business seasonal? Will it be affected by changes in the economy or society? What problems could your competitors create? Be realistic, honest and open about these potential problems, and make sure you understand the effects they could have on your business should they occur. Create a Plan B that can swing into action if necessary, and be ready to explain all this to potential funders – in fact it's best if you bring up the subject first. They will be impressed if you are well prepared in this area.

5. **A personality and style they can work with.** This is one area where funders can be ready to invest based on all the other factors, but won't if they simply don't like the person, or the team, running the business. Funders invest in the individual more than they invest in the business, so this is vitally important. Be careful not to come across as arrogant instead of confident, cocky instead of friendly and so on. Be as natural as possible; be calm, professional and friendly – if you try to play the big-shot they will quickly be deterred. A funder knows that an investment in your business is for the long term, and that they will have to work with you over a few

years at least. They will want to know that you are prepared to listen to their ideas and experience, and they will be keen to see that you are prepared to communicate openly with them. They will want to be sure that each meeting with you won't be a nightmare.

6. **The x-factor.** By this I don't mean that you want to appear on television and sing cover songs in a warbly voice before being criticized by Simon Cowell – I refer to the original idea after which they named the television show. Some people have something special about them that you just can't put your finger on. If you've ever met anyone famous (with real talent) you may have seen this at first-hand. You are keenly aware of their presence in a room through some kind of sixth sense, you are almost in awe of them, you automatically give them respect. Aside from the 'famous', you may know people like this in your industry. At social events people seem to cluster around them, they move around the room effortlessly as people make way for them. The x-factor is very hard, but not impossible, to develop if you don't have it naturally. If you don't have it, it's best just to work even harder at the other five things that funders look for.

However, if you do want to work towards developing the x-factor, then be aware that it is about calm confidence rather than cockiness, listening rather than speaking, making others feel important instead of letting them know how important you are, being directed towards a clear goal rather than frantically chasing anything that looks interesting, being led by your values rather than simply by money or fame. It's about being happy and friendly instead of maudlin and frosty, questioningly optimistic rather than determinedly sceptical, accepting of mistakes but demanding of quality, and many more attitudes and behaviours. If you want to find out more there are many motivational books on the subject, and you can also look out for my book, *How to be an Entrepreneur*, for more details specific to business owners.

Once funders see that you have at least most of those points within your management team, they will want to see that it all fits together to make an effective team.

Can you demonstrate how well you all get on, that everyone gets their chance to have a say, that difficult questions can be asked, and that the leader doesn't just steamroller over everyone else's ideas? Make sure that each of you makes a clear contribution to the pitch, whether in the documents or in the presentation itself. It should be evident that everyone gets a chance to add value to the team, and that the rest of the team value that input and respect the other team-members.

It is also valuable to have a mix of different types of people within the team. An effective team has a mix of big-picture people and detail people, dynamic let's-get-started people and thorough let's-get-finished people as well as others. It can really help to find out a little more about the different personality types, and perhaps even to test yourselves using one of the accepted psychometric testing methods, such as Belbin or Myers-Briggs.

Experienced funders will look for a good balance of people, a team that fits together to create something that is more powerful than simply the sum of its parts.

Special advice Seed or start-up

If you are a one-man band pitching for funding you will have to work harder. Funders will worry about the narrow range of experience available to the business, as well as the lack of discussion and different viewpoints around key decisions, so you will have to demonstrate that you have outside advice available to you (perhaps a mentor). Funders will also worry about what will happen when you are on holiday, sick, or if you get hit by a bus and the business suddenly has to cope without you. You need to demonstrate that you will have staff who are capable enough to run things in your absence. You may also need to have insurance in place that will pay out if you are unable to work. This is called key-man insurance and we will look at it in more depth later in the book.

Innocent Drinks, the fruit smoothie drink company, was started by three friends with proper careers, giving them complementary talents and experiences – but none of them in the drinks industry. They each have different personality types, and fit together well as a team.

Also, have you noticed yet how I referred to 'talent' rather than management, personnel, staff, etc.? This is something I learned from business guru Tom Peters, and it has stuck because it just seems so right. Musicians, actors and sports-people are often referred to as 'the talent'. This is because their job requires them to study, practise and practise repeatedly to remain at the top of their field – to be great at what they do. This isn't about qualifications or their CV, it's about how good they are.

The same should be true for you and your team. Recognize your talents for what they are and what they should be. Keep learning, keep sharpening these talents. An athlete who becomes the world's best in their field doesn't then stop training, they have to train harder because everyone wants to beat them, and so it should be with you. Work to be at the top of your game, and then work hard to stay there. This means reading books, going on courses, listening to training CDs, reading business and trade magazines, newsletters and websites. It means networking and listening to the industry gossip on the grapevine; and making sure that the rest of your team are developing their talents in the same way.

Opportunity

Next an investor will look at the opportunity you plan to pursue in your business – but note that I refer to 'opportunity' rather than simply 'idea'. An opportunity is more than just an idea, it's an idea that people want, and want enough to pay money for it.

Many entrepreneurs think that an idea alone is enough, and forget to look in detail at who might actually want to pay money for it, and whether the amount of money they would be prepared to pay will make the business worthwhile. It also doesn't need to be an invention, or anything brand new for you to be the first to market with. It just has to add a new twist that customers want and will pay money for.

USP

Funders will often ask, 'What is your USP?' This stands for unique selling point (or to some people, unique selling proposition) and means the new twist you add to an existing product or service that sets you apart from the competition.

The USP for Google, at least initially, was that they sorted the search results in order of their relevance to the customer's search query. This saved their users time, because the results they were most likely to want would be on the first page, while they could be browsing through pages and pages of randomly ordered results on other search engines. Of course, as it was a popular USP it was quickly copied, so Google has had to develop others such as the simple user interface, localized searches, etc.

The USP for Volvo cars is safety. Their customers select them in preference to other cars because of the extra safety features, and the feeling of solidness and security inside the car. As a result they are able to charge more than many other car manufacturers.

USPs are hotly contested in the competitive airline industry. One airline introduces flat beds in first class, the rest copy. One airline starts offering them in business class, the rest copy. Other airlines compete on the USP of really cheap fares, and constantly fight to be seen as cheaper than the others. Whether it's a feature or a price, a USP can sometimes only last a few weeks, so they have constantly to develop the next unique idea to attract customers.

What is your USP? Why will customers choose you over your competitors? Human beings are known for their inertia, their resistance to change, so if you are going to offer them something new, you'll have to show that you have a very good enticement to encourage them even to try you out.

Funders will be paying a lot of attention to your USP, to be certain that it really is unique, and that it really is a selling point – so you should pay a lot of attention to identifying it and working out how to communicate it clearly and simply.

Business model

Once a funder is convinced that you have the talent, have an opportunity and have a USP, they will want to know more about your business model. This is the way in which you will capitalize on your talent and the opportunity to generate income, how you will deliver the product or service, and how you will maximize the profit from the income. You might think this is obvious: you'll tell the customer what you do, they'll buy it, you'll give it to them and they'll give you money – but there is much more to it than that.

Case studies

Let's use Google as an example again. Have you ever searched on Google? Yes? Have you ever paid them any money for the search results you got? No? Well, how on earth are they so profitable? What you've missed is that you think the search results, or the search engine, is the product or service they are selling. In truth, *you* are what they are selling. When you looked at the page with the search results, there were advertisements on it, and a proportion of the users click on them. They then charge the advertiser for that click. Their business model is to provide a service to attract users, and then sell those users to other companies. *You* are their product.

Another example is Hewlett Packard. When you buy a printer from them for around £70, do you think that's the deal done, and they've made all the profit they need to from that? No, there's not much profit at all in that £70 and rumour has it that sometimes there's even a loss once they've given a big trade discount to the retailers and paid for marketing, distribution, packaging and the parts and labour to make the thing. Their business model is that you will buy ink or toner cartridges from them every few months for the next two or three years, at between £10 and £90 a time depending on the type of printer. There's a lot of profit in the charge for the cartridges and that's where they make their money. Their business model is based around the plan that customers feel they are getting a bargain when they buy a printer for £70, and then they are locked in to buying the ink cartridges.

▶

Contrary to popular belief, Nike doesn't make trainers. Nike's business model is to focus its energy on the areas where it has most expertise and can add most value – it builds its brand, designs and sells trainers – but it doesn't do the bit in the middle, the actual manufacture. It has suppliers in countries where labour is cheap who make the actual product under contract to Nike. Anyone can make trainers, but only Nike can put the Nike brand on them, design them to meet their customers' needs, or sell them to Nike approved retailers. Those are the parts of the business model that make a pair of trainers that cost less than £1 to make sell at prices anywhere upwards of £50.

Tesco (and the other supermarket chains) have a business model that relies on using their immense buying power to negotiate lower prices and longer payment terms from their suppliers. Their customers then pay when they take the goods away from the store, often within a couple of days of the products being delivered to Tesco. They then invest that money for the remaining 80 or so days until they have to pay their suppliers. They earn a lot of interest on this money, and it is a large slice of their profits. In recent years they have developed this even further, by coming up with the idea of lending this money back to their customers! So you can now get Tesco credit cards, Tesco loans and so on. This earns them much higher interest (between 7 per cent and 20 per cent depending on whether it's a loan or credit card) than they would be paid for investing the money in the financial markets.

These are just some of the varieties of business models available. As you can see, there are a number of elements that can be tweaked to develop *your* ideal business model and set you apart from the competition. Your business model can be a great competitive advantage.

Your business model will take into account:

- each of your customer 'audiences';
- what each of them wants;

- who you can charge and what you can charge them for;

- how much they are willing to pay;

- how they pay that money to you;

- how you maximize the cash flow advantages of that money once you have it;

- what work you will do inside the company, and what you will get suppliers to do;

- how you will pay and control those suppliers;

- how you will protect your company's specialist position, knowledge and brand.

Surf the trends

In making sure that your idea really is an opportunity, funders will take into consideration current trends – and you should do so too. Be aware of what is happening in society, in politics and the economy, and use these trends to your advantage. Keep your eyes open, read a variety of newspapers and magazines, listen to what people are talking about and look for patterns. Could these be part of a wider trend? How will your business surf these trends and turn them to your advantage? How will you mitigate any detrimental effects?

Special advice Early stage, growth or turnaround

Just because you are already trading with an existing product range, existing sales materials and so on, it doesn't mean that you can relax, thinking you've got this section covered. It really *is* worth taking the time to do a complete review of the opportunity you have chosen to pursue, whether you have a suitable USP, whether you have the best business model, and what the trends are in your industry. Perhaps it is worth getting out to speak to some of your customers if you've been a bit removed from the sharp end of your business for a while. You are very likely to be surprised by what you find, or be inspired to new and better ideas.

Planning

If you have the right talent, and you have a good opportunity, then you have overcome the two biggest hurdles. But funders will then look to see that you have developed a suitable plan to capitalize on the opportunity, continue to develop the talent and manage the money.

Physically, this will take the form of a business plan that includes a brief summary of the company's development and work to date if applicable.

An outline of the target market will also be required, preferably with details of specific customers ready to buy, along with details of how you will sell to this target market, what they will pay, etc. You should also provide brief summaries of the relevant experience and background of the management team and key staff.

However, the funders will want to see a level of planning that goes beyond this written plan. They will be reading between the lines, and asking questions to ascertain whether you really have researched and do understand the market and the opportunity, that you really do have the talent and that you have the systems and procedures in the business to work effectively. One thing of which they will be absolutely certain is that the business won't go according to your plan. It may be better, it may be worse, you may even arrive at the same end result – but you won't get there in the same way.

Someone I know who used to be in the army tells me that they have a saying, 'No plan survives the first encounter with the enemy.' No matter how carefully you research and develop your plan, people are people and will do something unpredictable. You are relying on your suppliers, your customers, your staff, yourself and many, many others. There is so much that cannot be predicted. Because of this, investors will want to see that – even though you have absolute confidence that you can achieve Plan A – you have Plans B, C and even D tucked away just in case. They will ask you what you would do if sales were down 20 per cent on your forecasts, what you would do if a key customer stopped buying from you, if a key member of staff left, if a key supplier went bust and so on. They will look for any possible challenge you may face. The main tick in the box they are looking for at this stage is that you have realized that these things can happen, that you have thought about them, that you have taken some steps to minimize the risks of these occurring and that you have some kind of fall-back plan. They will be instantly deterred if you simply try to convince them that none of these things will happen.

Sales plan

A business plan is generally used to present your company to outsiders, and after that it typically gets put in a drawer and forgotten about. This worries funders, who will be concerned that without careful attention to the plan you will drift off course. To show that you really will put your plan into action, it's worth developing mini-plans for each area of the business – the key one being a sales plan. Draw out the sales plan and expectations from the main business plan and create a special plan for use by your salespeople, and by you in monitoring their work. Break down the key milestones into smaller milestones. What do your sales need to be each week? How many new prospects do you need to find, research and contact? How many prospects should turn into customers? What advertising do you need to do to create these prospects? What PR? What other marketing activity will generate new business? What are the time-lines for these to happen? Keep the plan short and to the point. That way it will be easier to follow in everyday working life.

Funders will look for evidence like this to reassure themselves that you have a plan for putting your ideas, research and strategy into action to make your business plan reality. They want to know that the business plan isn't just to impress them – it's for you to use in building your business.

Critical success factors

When you run a business there are so many things to think about and do that it's easy to lose track of what is really important. Funders have seen this happen, and they will be looking for evidence that you won't fall into this trap. They want to see that you can focus on the parts of your plan that really matter.

These parts are known as the critical success factors. What are the few things that would make the difference between success or failure if they do or do not occur? These might be getting regulatory or standards approval for a key new product in a specialist industry, winning the custom of a key distributor, retaining certain key members of staff, keeping costs below a certain level, being able to sell at a certain price and so on. Funders will be impressed if you have identified the critical success factors for your business, and intend to focus your efforts on making sure they happen to plan.

Competitors

The next thing that investors will be looking for is a healthy respect for your competitors. This includes companies already in the market and companies who may enter the market when you launch your new venture and signpost an opportunity they may have missed.

Funders will be instantly deterred if you simply bad mouth the competition, or dismiss them. Do **not** say:

- 'Bigcorp are idiots. They'll never spot this opportunity, and even if they do they won't know how to respond.'

- 'Smallcorp are fly-by-nights. They don't have the resources or the skills to do this properly, customers will soon see through them.'

- 'Thingummy PLC's products are rubbish.'

- 'We have no competition, our product/service is unique.' This is one of the most common phrases that funders hear, and they've given up laughing at it. It really irritates them now. You always have competition. Even if there aren't products or services quite like yours, customers do not have an unlimited supply of money and will have to make a choice between your product and something else they may want to buy. Even if McDonald's didn't have competition from other burger chains, they would have competition from kebab shops, chip shops, sandwich shops and even newsagents selling chocolate bars. They are in the 'I need something quick and tasty to fill me up now' market, not just the burger market.

Even if your competitors' products really aren't as good as yours, there are plenty of examples of how a better product lost out to a lesser product from a competitor:

- BSB had a satellite TV system that offered better quality reception on a much smaller satellite dish – but Sky had the football rights and won the satellite TV wars.

- Betamax was a much better quality video format – and is still used by professional TV cameramen and engineers to this day – but it lost out to VHS because VHS had a better marketing campaign.

- Richard Branson developed a lottery game with more money going to good causes, and better odds of winning, but lost the British lottery franchise bid to Camelot PLC, because the regulator preferred continuity (like so many customers!).

If you don't respect your competitors, and see them as people who are just as smart – if not smarter – than you, and probably have more resources, people and money than you, then you are heading for a fall. They will outspend you on marketing, offer better incentives to distributors and so on.

If you are competing with an existing company entrenched in your target market then things are even more difficult. Customers are very resistant to change. Even if they are not happy with company A, they will wait to see what happens with your company before jumping ship. They will worry that you won't be as good as you say you are, or that you'll go bust. It's so ironic that customers will complain continuously about a company, so that a competitor will enter the market. Customers wait to see if it will stay in business before giving it their business, and – sure enough – it goes out of business. I've seen it happen before and it will happen again. Never underestimate how attached to the competition your target customers are.

Funders will expect you to be well aware of who your competitors really are. Don't be fooled into having too narrow a view of your competitors – remember my point about McDonald's.

If you are launching a web design agency, then as well as competing against similar agencies you are also competing against:

- a family member or friend of the customer who is 'good at computers' and will do it on the cheap;

- other marketing materials the customer can decide to spend their budget on instead of a website – leaflets, advertising, PR, etc.

If you are opening a shop, then you will not only be competing with other shops selling the same things but also with other shops in the area.

The customer has a limited amount of cash – do they spend that on something from your shop, or on a really nice set of saucepans they've seen in Debenhams down the road?

Take some time to think about the wider range of competitors that you are up against. This sort of thinking will impress your potential funders.

Once you know who your competitors really are, you need to find out as much as possible about them and consider how you measure up against them. Do plenty of research. Your local reference library can help with some of this, but you can also find a lot of the answers on the web – including on your competitors' own websites. These are some of the things you may want to find out:

- Who the key management and staff are in the company and their backgrounds.

- Their product range, including features and benefits of each.

- The price list.

- How sales are going for each product.

- The sales channels they use to reach their customers.

- The suppliers they use.

- Their main customers, and some idea of why those customers buy from them.

- The financial standing of the business.

- How the industry views this company – are they respected, reviled or do they go un-noticed?

It is also well worth doing some mystery shopping and buying your competitors' products to try. Make notes on the whole experience. What were the staff like, how was their service, how efficient were they? What sort of range did they have, what's the product like, is it good quality, how did they price their range? And so on. Get chatting to the staff if possible, it's amazing what you can learn if you let them talk. How is business – are they busy or slow? What stuff sells? Are there customer complaints about anything?

For each of your close competitors, create a file and write up your research. Keep updating it with press clippings, printouts from the web, new industry gossip, etc. For each of your more general competitors – for example, other industries that may be in indirect competition with you, create a folder for the whole industry. File away any industry statistics or trends, clippings from trade magazines, etc., and keep these folders up to date over time. Your funders will be very impressed if you can talk about this research and perhaps even quote from it in your business plan, your presentation or your answers to their questions. This will send out all the right messages about your taking the competition seriously.

The stage beyond this is to try to anticipate the next steps that your competitors will take. They won't be standing still. They will have new products, services, promotions or marketing tactics in development. What could these be? What would you be doing if you were in their shoes? Also, they won't ignore your entry into the market. If you come on to their radar in any way – perhaps if a customer switches to you – then they will react. What will they do? Increase marketing? Drop prices? Spread bad rumours about you? What else could they do? How would you respond in each of these situations?

Think very carefully about what your competitors are most likely to do AND what would cause the most damage to you. Assume that they are much cleverer than you. If you plan for the worst, you can only be pleasantly surprised. Paying serious attention to your competitors in this way will impress potential funders. It's rarely done – even by long-established successful businesses – which is why companies that have been around for decades can go out of business because of an innovation by their competitors that they didn't expect and are too late to react to.

Make sure your funders can see, in your business plan or your presentation, that you have taken the time to identify your competitors, research them and anticipate their next moves.

Special advice Seed, start-up or early stage

The very first stages of a business can be chaotic and you spend all your time just doing what has to be done. But it really can make a huge difference to your efficiency and your stress levels if you take the time to put a few proper plans in place, and a few systems/procedures to support them.

Many of the most successful entrepreneurial businesses adopted a big company attitude even when they were very small – making sure the proper contracts were in place, that people understood what their jobs were and how to do them, and so on.

The best way to achieve this, whenever you do something for the first time that is likely to be repeated, is to do it in such a way that it can be re-used. For instance, when you send out a covering letter with a brochure to a customer, save the letter as a template, so the next time you need it you can just drop in the next customer's name and address.

The same goes for contracts and every other piece of paperwork.

It can also help to have a regular monthly meeting for all of your management – even if that's just you – to review progress against the plan and look at any corrections that need to be made.

WHAT FUNDERS LOOK FOR IN THE 'DEAL'

Once a funder has decided that they are interested in providing funding for your business – whether in the form of a loan, investment in equity or any of the other options – they will look to see that the deal can meet their financial requirements for such investments. These will include how much money they will eventually be able to earn back from the money they put into your business, how much risk is involved and what protection they will have from that risk. Finally they will want to see *how* they will get their money back. For a loan this is obvious, as it will be paid back over time, but equity investors will need an 'exit', allowing them to sell their shares.

Funding requirements

Some funders won't even consider small amounts – it's simply not worth their time. Other funders focus only on smaller amounts, and don't have the resources to finance large deals. Other funders focus on particular sectors, providing funding only to technology companies, or start-ups, or management buy-outs, etc. Therefore you have to make sure you are pitching your idea to the right kind of funder, for the right kind of funding. We'll look at this in more detail later.

Level of risk

A funder will then examine what the level of risk is in the business and the investment you are asking for. They will have a fairly good idea of this from your business plan, but they will want to conduct further enquiries. For a lender this is likely to involve conducting credit searches on the company and its key directors. For an equity investor it may involve 'due diligence'.

For a small investment this process will be fairly basic. A funder may want to:

- speak to one or two of your customers or potential customers;

- see your company accounts;

- speak to other references such as your accountant, other directors, suppliers, etc.;

- try out your products or services;

- check that you have the correct insurances (see below).

For larger equity investments, and some large debt finance, the due diligence may also involve checking:

- all your staff contracts to make sure that key staff are tied in as much as possible;

- agreements or contracts with customers to ensure that the prices and contract period are agreed, stable and sustainable;

- agreements or contracts with suppliers;

- any trademarks or patents that protect your products or brands;

- the existence and value of any assets that you claim ownership of, such as vehicles;

- whether there are any disputes with staff, suppliers, customers or other third parties – these may lead to costly court cases, settlements or large legal fees later;

- that you are up to date with payments to suppliers and HM Revenue and Customs;

- that you are up to date with collecting payments from customers;

- . . . and much more – they will check every relevant fact about your business.

Due diligence on large funding deals can be very, very thorough. Make sure that you have absolutely no skeletons in your closet, or that you have been honest about them – they will be found; and if you haven't been honest the funders will worry about what else you are hiding.

Once they have done their research, the funder will come to a view on what level of risk there is in investing in your company.

The risks that the funder will consider include the following:

- Is the company too reliant on one or two key people (perhaps you)?

- If so, what has been done to lock those people in and ensure their commitment?

- Is the company's USP protected in any way or can it be easily copied?

- Will the management team cope when things don't go to plan?

- Is there going to be sufficient finance in the business to achieve the plan?

- Will the cash flow in the business be manageable?

- Will larger existing competitors launch an offensive against you?

- Will customers actually buy what you plan to sell?

- Will other suppliers quickly copy you and steal your market?

- Have you and your management team got the commitment and drive to see this through?

- Is this company a personal plaything for you the entrepreneur, or will you let it grow and flourish even if that means a change of role for you or a change in direction from your original idea?

- Will there be a suitable exit for the funder? (More on this later, see p. 36.)

Protection against risk

Now that the funder is aware of the risks in your proposal, they will seek to minimize the potential impact of those risks on their investment. This can be done by persuading the business to put proper contracts in place and insure against key risks, or in the case of debt finance obtaining security against the debt, such as a mortgage over property or other assets or personal guarantees.

Contracts

Funders will want you to tie in your key management and staff with good solid contracts that will also protect your trade secrets and sales contacts if a member of staff leaves to work for the competition. They will also want you to tie your key customers into as long-term a relationship as possible, giving the business security in the short term, and plenty of notice if the customer ever plans to drop you as a supplier, although this won't always be possible or applicable.

Insurances

If there are a few key people in the business, most funders would like the company to have insurance that will pay out if these people die or are unable to work through illness. This is often called 'key man' insurance, but it is essentially just a life and critical illness insurance policy with the business as the beneficiary. This means that if you go under the number 32 bus tomorrow, the business receives a large cash lump sum, and can either pay back its debts, pay a lump sum to shareholders and close down, or use the money to recruit a replacement and fund the business in the meantime.

If you have a number of different shareholders in the company then funders may ask you to put in place life insurance on these people. This is because if a shareholder dies, their shares will pass to their next of kin. The next of kin can then do what they like with them (unless otherwise specified in a good shareholders' agreement, which we'll talk about in more detail below). They could sell them to your competitors or, if they inherit enough shares, they could force a change to the board of directors and put themselves on the board to cause havoc in the company, or to force the sale of the company. However, if the company has been paid a large amount of money on the death of the shareholder because of the insurance policy, you can easily afford to buy back the shares, ensuring the shareholder's successor is looked after but the company avoids any potentially difficult situations.

Indemnities and warranties

This applies principally when you are raising the funding to buy an existing business. In this case your funders will want to see that you have obtained warranties or indemnities from the previous owners, so that they have the risk of any problems that occur as a result of anything prior to the date of the transfer of ownership. Thus, for example, if you find that HM Revenue and Customs are knocking on your door a few months after the sale saying they are owed tens of thousands of pounds in overdue taxes, you can simply force the previous owners to pay.

Personal guarantees

If you are seeking debt finance or taking on another major commitment such as a lease, and you are running a limited company, the lender may ask you and other directors to give personal guarantees. This is because the limited company protects you from personal liability (unless you have done something illegal or severely wrong in your role as director, in which case a court may hold you liable). If the business runs into trouble, the funder will want to be able to claim the debt from you personally. We'll talk more about personal guarantees in Chapter 8.

Other security

If the business has any assets of value, such as property, cash, machinery and so on, lenders are likely to want to take a 'charge' over these assets as security for any loan. A charge is like the mortgage on your house, and means that if you fail to repay the money the lender can seize the assets concerned and sell them. A charge can be limited to a particular asset such as a property, or a machine. Invoice finance, which we shall discuss later, is lending secured by a charge over your debtor book – the money that people owe your business.

Shareholders' agreement

As I mentioned earlier, if one of your shareholders dies, their shares pass to the estate of the deceased and then on to their successors. The estate and the successors can do what they like with the shares, unless your shareholders have agreed in writing to a clearly defined procedure on their death. This is likely to state that the shareholder's estate must offer to sell the shares back to the company at a price decided by an independent valuation of the business at the time. Only if the company turns down this offer can the estate retain the shares or sell them to anyone else. A shareholders' agreement will also protect against other potential problems and set out how any disputes between the shareholders will be resolved.

Any funder who will be buying equity in your business is likely to want a good shareholders' agreement to be in place.

Return on investment

If a funder can satisfy themselves that the level of risk in the business is acceptable, and that suitable steps have been taken to offset that risk, they will then seek to ensure that they will get the level of return on their investment that they require. Return on investment is the reward that they look for in return for the risk they are taking on by providing you with funding.

Lenders

Debt financiers typically look for a low-risk profile, and therefore the rewards are relatively low. You will typically pay interest on the debt at an agreed rate (probably between 2 and 4 per cent) above the Bank of England base rate. You may also have to pay fees for arranging the debt, taking security and pretty much anything else you can think of.

Equity investors

Equity investors are willing to accept a higher level of risk – but they are therefore also looking for higher levels of reward. If they invested their money in gilt edged bonds – very low risk – they could expect a return on investment of about 5 per cent a year. If they invested their money in blue chip companies on the stock market – higher risk – they could expect a return of about 10–14% a year on average. So it stands to reason that an equity investor will be looking for a higher reward than that for the increased risk that your business represents. Just how high is determined by the level of risk, the duration of the investment and what kind of equity investors they are. An average to work on is about 20% annual return, but some venture capitalists may insist on an annual return even higher than this.

Exit

This is the method by which the funder will be able to get their money back and realize their return on investment. For small amounts of debt finance such as standard loans or overdrafts this is simple – you pay the money back over an agreed period with interest. For equity finance involving some business angels it may still be quite simple. They might be happy earning dividends (once your company is profitable) and continuing to be part of your company. Otherwise, the amounts involved may be small and you might be able to raise debt finance to buy them out, providing their exit and giving you a greater stake in your company.

For most equity finance and more complicated debt finance it is likely to involve selling your business in one way or another.

- **A trade sale** involves selling your business to another company, probably in your industry. This could be a competitor, a supplier or a company that wants to enter your market.

- **An initial public offering** (IPO) lists your business on one of the equity markets (probably OFEX or AIM), and sells your shares to investors in that market. These could be institutions or private investors. You end up with lots more shareholders, but with each of them having a smaller stake.

- **A management buy-out** (MBO) is where you and/or your fellow management team raise the finance to buy the whole business, exiting the other investors. This will usually be financed by a debt financier, a venture capital firm or a combination.

- **A management buy-in** (MBI) is selling your business to a new team of executives backed by financiers.

- **A buy-in management buy-out** (BIMBO – seriously, I'm not kidding!) is a mix of the two previous options, with a new executive or executives buying into the business alongside your existing management team to bring extra experience ready for growth. This might be particularly appropriate if you have decided to exit the company too.

- **Refinancing** involves selling the business to a new financial investor (probably a venture capital firm), exiting the previous investor(s).

Be aware that securing a substantial equity investment into your business sets the clock ticking on the sale of your company. Your funders will want you to have thought through the options for exiting them, and to understand what it means to you. They will also want some idea of the timescale in which you plan to exit them.

3

CHAPTER THREE

Preparing your business for a funding round

The first step in raising money for your company is to find out what shape your business is in now – and then examine how to get it into the right shape to attract funding. I know this step can be frustrating for entrepreneurs – you just want to rush ahead and get on with actually asking for the money – but it is a really important step to take. If you do this work now you'll avoid looking an idiot in front of a powerful investor who will only give you one chance to make your case.

The truth, and nothing but the truth

There's no point in kidding yourself at this stage of the process, because the investors you are pitching to later will be intelligent and experienced, and will quickly spot what you have glossed over. It's far better to be honest about any problems now and work out a solution. By doing this thinking in advance you will avoid embarrassing moments when you present your business to investors.

It does take courage to be this honest with yourself, however, particularly if you are raising money because your business hasn't been going as well as you hoped. But I urge you to bring all the skeletons out of the cupboard and do something about them. If you approach the funding process like this then your business will be in better shape, as well as better funded, by the end of it – and that means you'll be burning fuel more efficiently.

OPPORTUNITY

A healthy business requires a good opportunity. I use the word 'opportunity' deliberately in a place where other books refer to a business having a good 'idea', because we need to think beyond the idea. A business idea is a thought you have had for a product or service you could provide. An opportunity is the next step – it is an idea that people are willing to pay you money for.

At a very early stage in your pitch funders will want proof that you have a good opportunity, which means they will be more interested in your business if you have customers who have already paid you money for your idea, or whom you have lined up ready to pay you money for your idea. This proof is crucial. So what can you show them?

If you run an existing business this will be easier, unless the funding you seek is for expansion into a new area. You can show them lists of your customers, amounts that these customers have paid and testimonials from happy customers. This will press all the right buttons.

If you run a start-up business, or are planning new products or services, you need to work harder to provide this evidence. Do not try to gloss over any lack of proof, as that approach will ring alarm bells with the funders and they will quickly lose interest. And lack of proof should ring alarm bells with you too, as you will be investing huge amounts of time in this opportunity, and perhaps quite a bit of money as well. It really is worth spending some time now to find that proof, or to learn that you need to develop a new opportunity instead. At this stage you won't lose money, and you won't lose face in front of the funders, if you find out you got it wrong.

So what proof do you need? Simple. Sales.

This can be difficult if what you plan to offer customers is complicated or expensive to make in even small numbers, but do try to develop some kind of prototype. Otherwise come up with a clear way to demonstrate what your product will be able to do.

Special advice Seed or start-up

If you're planning a start-up it's even better if you can run your business in a small way at first, perhaps in your spare time, demonstrating that you can earn money from it. This does mean that it will take longer to launch your business properly and you won't earn much money from it for a while, but it will be a much better business and you will be able to negotiate a much better deal on the finance – making you more money in the long run. In the United States it's much more common for people to have a full-time job, but run their own business in the evenings and at weekends. This is a great idea that can give you a real head start in your business with less risk. Don't rush to give up the day job too soon.

If you run an existing business it may be easier – perhaps you already have customers who might also like to buy this new product or service. Go and ask them. Get their input, their feedback and a pledge to do business with you.

Some customers – more than you might imagine – may even be prepared to place orders in advance, although they may need some incentive unless your product is very exclusive. However, it is well worth offering a discount in this situation as it could be a key element in helping you raise finance. It has been known for customers to place an order and pay in advance to help a new business get off the ground. Don't be too shy to ask – a bit of cheek could get you a cheque! Wouldn't it be nice to get the finance you need for your business from your customer at the same time as your first order? It happens all the time, even for start-ups that haven't launched yet.

Special advice Turnaround

You're going to have to work hard to show funders why your business really does have a good opportunity when it has got into trouble. You'll have to either steer the company towards a new opportunity, or find some solid evidence that shows the opportunity is there, and is worthwhile – but the company has been approaching it in the wrong way. The business hasn't been working – so something has to change. Explain what that is.

Market research

If there is no way you can get a few definite sales under your belt before raising finance then it's well worth approaching some target customers to gauge their interest. This is true market research, in place of the picture many people have in their head of standing on street corners with a clipboard. The best way to develop this research is by starting with some imaginary customers to create target customer profiles. I describe this more fully in *The Small Business Handbook*, but the idea is to imagine between three and five fictional customers in detail, with each one representing a type of real customer in your business. If they are individuals, make up a name for them, and make up information about their hobbies, lifestyle, family, holidays and anything else that helps you understand who they are and what motivates them. If they are companies, profile the individual who will be your key contact within each company. Put in more detail about what they do, what the company does, who their customers are, who the other key contacts and decision makers in the company are (make up names again), what their key motivating factors are in any deal, how they do business, etc. Make the profiles as detailed as possible, so that you and your team can refer to them by name, and picture them in your mind, whenever you are trying to categorize a new customer or make key decisions on new products or services. You should know these people as if they are your friends.

In this way you can identify who your key target customer types are for your service. Next you need to work out how to find customers in each of these categories:

- Can they simply be searched for on the web or in the business phone directory (i.e. if you sell to estate agents, or accountants)?

- What places can they regularly be found in (consumers in coffee shops, town centres, the gym, etc.)?

- What events will they go to? (Business people may go to networking events, trade shows, conferences.)

- Who do you know who might know these kind of people?

If you will be selling to businesses, you can use your answers to these questions to do some research to build up lists of potential customers in each category. Next you can contact these people to conduct your market research.

If you will be selling to consumers, you can consider the following:

1. Do the clipboard thing. Design a questionnaire and get out in the right places to meet your potential customers and ask them questions. It can be difficult to get the answers you need from this kind of research as most people are reluctant to stop, and those who do may not be the kind of people who can provide the answers you need!

2. Organize a focus group. Invite people to your workplace, a rented meeting room, or a cafe, for a drink and a chat about your ideas. You can get friends to invite people, put up a notice inviting people, etc. This gives much more time to explore people's reactions in detail – but it can be difficult to get them to give up their spare time.

3. Conduct telephone research. This can be soul destroying. You don't like being contacted on your home phone by someone you've never met, and nor does anyone else.

4. Conduct door-to-door surveys. This is better than doing surveys on the phone, but you still need to be prepared for the 'No'.

5. Post or email questionnaires to people. This has the disadvantage that you can't chat to them about their responses, or pick up any 'between the lines' messages from the way they speak or their reaction.

Whether they are business customers or consumers, if they are genuinely interested in what you might be able to offer them then they will be more than happy to spend some time answering your questions about what their needs are. You will want to know:

- who currently supplies them with any similar product or service;

- how much they pay (they may not tell you this);

- how much of this product or service they buy, and how often;

- what are the most important considerations to them when buying? (Try to dig deeper than price. Although they'll always try to negotiate a cheaper deal, you'll often find that they're willing to pay more for quality or reliability. I know I am in my business.)

Alternatively, you can commission external agencies to conduct your market research for you – and if you are a sizeable existing company this may be the first thing you think of – but I recommend that you and your staff get out there to meet your customers and potential customers yourselves. Only you can pick up on the real unspoken reactions, only you know enough about your idea to pick up on the important objections or suggestions from people. As well as questioning representatives of all your customer types you can do research into statistics and trends that relate to them and their purchases. Your local reference library will be able to help, or you can search online – Google is one of the best resources for entrepreneurs!

When you get the results of your customer research it's vital to actually analyze it and use the results that you have collected to get your business into shape. You may find that customers want a slightly different service, want to buy in different pack sizes, don't need all the features you are offering and so on. By listening to your customers you may be able to charge more, or save on your costs. You may be able to sell more units, or manufacture more efficiently. Your customers can give you so many ideas for improving what you do – if you just listen to them and act on their feedback.

Is the pricing right?

Getting the pricing right is a key part of maximizing your opportunity.

One of the most common mistakes that entrepreneurs make is to get the pricing of their product or service wrong – and they generally set their prices too low! We're all very modest and don't believe we are worth so much money – so we set the prices as low as we possibly can. I'm frequently asked about pricing by entrepreneurs, and I always end up suggesting that their prices are too low.

One entrepreneur I advised was a specialist in a particular field of web design. He was about to launch a consultancy to offer his specialist advice to internet design companies. There was a lot of interest and he was trying to work out what to charge. He rang me up for advice because he was very worried that the £25 an hour he planned to charge was too expensive. I suggested he needed to be charging about £150 an hour and he nearly fainted. He still didn't take my advice and started by charging £50 an hour. Eventually he got feedback from customers, and found out what they were charging his services on at – and he put his prices up to £150 an hour. His business is now very successful and growing very fast as he recruits new consultants to work for him. The strange thing is that he is getting more work now he is more expensive, because people think he must be very good to be able to charge those prices. If you do a quick bit of mental arithmetic you'll see how much extra profit he is making per month as a result of charging the right price for the opportunity.

If your prices are too low, some customers won't believe that what you are offering is good quality, or that you will provide a good service. They will be suspicious of what the 'catch' is. Have you heard the phrase 'reassuringly expensive'? I recommend that it's what you aim for.

Of course, every business is different, and easyJet wouldn't be where it is now if it was 'reassuringly expensive', but there are customers who won't fly on the cheap budget airlines because they worry that aircraft maintenance might be one of the things that is being cut back to permit the low prices. There will always be customers looking for a bargain, and you can do very well by serving that market, but it is much more difficult to build a successful business in that market without a lot of finance behind you to help you negotiate equally cheap deals with your suppliers by buying in bulk.

Generally I believe it's better for entrepreneurs to leave the cheap and cheerful end of the market to the big companies who can only fight it out on price, and head for the more discerning end of the market where the requirements are quality, luxury and service. This is the end of the market the big companies have problems serving. But this is only my opinion, and quite a few entrepreneurs have proved, and will continue to prove, me wrong. However, there are numerous case studies of great, profitable and lasting companies that focus on a niche at the high end of the market.

Case study

Porsche is one of the best known brands in motoring – but it's also one of the smallest car manufacturers in the world. It sells 88,000 cars a year, but is so profitable (it is the most profitable car manufacturer in the world) that it has recently been able to buy a 20 per cent stake in Volkswagen for £2.2bn *in cash*. Meanwhile, Volkswagen sells 5.1 million cars a year, but still doesn't make a profit on its main VW brand. Which company would you rather be, the one that produces expensive cars for a niche market, or the one that produces cheaper cars for the mass market?

So, do take the time to examine the pricing of your products or services. Any rise in prices will go straight to your bottom line – that means it is all profit. Increasing your prices does not generally increase your costs, and therefore a small increase in price can make a very big difference to the success of your business. But how do you work out what the right price is?

The best method is through testing. Run adverts that offer your product for sale at different prices. Which one generates the most profit from the sales it makes? Remember that it's better to sell a bit less volume at a higher price than a bit more volume at a lower price. Profit is the only measure that matters.

A similar kind of testing can be done through other sales channels – but be careful not to risk one customer finding out that they paid a lot more than their friend for the same thing. Run the tests in different places if possible.

You can also research the prices that your competitors charge for similar products. Do you want to beat them on price, match them on price, or show that you are better by charging more?

You also need to know what the item is costing you. How much does the product, or its components and the labour required to assemble them, cost? Remember to include the costs of labour directly attributable to production of that product or service. So, if you run a web design company and you subcontract work to a freelancer, your costs include whatever you pay the freelancer.

Once you have covered the costs of producing the thing you are selling, you then need to factor in the other costs of your business such as premises, electricity, cleaning, computers, machinery and so on. If you expect to produce 20,000 items a year, and your overheads cost you £100,000 a year, then you will need to earn £5 from each item to contribute to the running costs of your business. On top of this you also need to earn a profit – what is left after every single cost in your business has been covered. A combination of all these factors will help you to determine the right price for your services.

If you're a bit nervous at the idea of starting with a high price, it's worth considering setting a higher price, and then running special offers and discounts as an introduction to attract customers to what you do – but be sure to emphasize that they are special offers, and what the real price is. It is much harder to raise your prices if you find out they are too low than to reduce your prices if they are too high.

For more in-depth help with pricing, I recommend the book *Smarter Pricing* by Tony Cram, published by Financial Times Prentice Hall.

Moving up from products to service to knowledge to community

If your business opportunity is focused around making, distributing or selling a product (or products), then you can further maximize your opportunity by adding services into your business plan.

The idea is that when you have a customer who is buying from you, it is much easier to 'up-sell' them to additional services around the product than it is to sell more products to completely new customers. Also, if you get a reputation for providing good service on top of simply selling products, word will soon spread and customers will flock to you.

Suitable services to add on would be:

- delivery;

- installation;

- a contract for regular scheduled maintenance;

- a contract for unscheduled emergency maintenance.

Many businesses have already moved from simply selling products to selling products AND services, so the next stage is to up-sell knowledge as well, for instance:

- training on how to use the products;

- consultancy to help select the right products;

- seminars on related subjects.

And there is a step beyond this, which very few business-people pay any attention to – you can up-sell a customer to community:

- A club for the kind of people who use your products or services (so a shop that sells outdoor gear may start an 'adventurers' club', holding regular meetings to offer previews of the latest products and chat about people's trips, as well as perhaps organizing an annual challenge and so on).

- A newsletter that's about more than just your company, it's about the industry, or the interest area of your customers.

- Events for your industry or your customers. Get them together to network or share knowledge.

In some cases you may decide to provide this community element free, as part of your marketing activity, but you'll find it will be more highly valued by customers if you charge for it.

If you run the community, you put yourself at the centre of things for your customers, and potentially in your industry.

So many business owners would be tempted to diversify by offering more and more products for different types of customer, but you take the same customers and sell them products, services, knowledge and community – all around the same opportunity. This also helps to lock in customers, because they are getting such a comprehensive service from you that no one else can match, and you are the gatekeeper to the community. Funders will be attracted by this smart approach, and be pleased that you are maximizing the opportunity while remaining focused.

So, we've seen that preparing your business opportunity for a funding round is about proving that you have the right opportunity through sales and/or market research, setting the price correctly and building on the opportunity while remaining focused.

TALENT

As we saw in Chapter 2, you don't just need the right opportunity, you need to ensure that you have the right talent available to take advantage of it.

Getting this right is absolutely vital to raising funding, because the funders realize it is crucial to the success of your business.

Special advice Seed or start-up

At this size, the talent may just be you. This won't be too much of a problem if you only need to raise a very small amount of funding, perhaps from friends and family or a bank. But if you want to raise larger amounts you will need to develop the business so that it doesn't rely entirely on you, or at least show how the funding will help you to achieve that.

Another hurdle in a new business is to show why you have the right talent to make this company work. What skills and experience do you have?

If you run an existing business that is seeking funding then you have already had a chance to prove that you really do have the talent on board. Find a way to demonstrate this proof within your business plan and your presentation. If this is an area in which your business has been lacking until now, put extra focus on getting it right.

Your management team

In a growing business it is important to spread the responsibility for the running of the company between a team of people with complementary skills. If a growing business relies on just one person it can very easily get out of control. Is there anyone within the business that you can help to move up to a management role? Do you need to recruit outside the business, or bring in a specialist adviser?

Funders will want to see that you have someone experienced who is clearly and confidently in charge of the finances. Next they will be keen to see that someone is in charge of sales, and that someone is in charge of making the products or delivering the service.

In an ideal world, none of these would be the entrepreneur. You would be in charge of these people, and your job would be to lead the business as a whole. But in the early years of growth of the business, the chances are that one or more of these roles will be taken by you, as well as the job of running the company as a whole. In this case you need to show that you have a plan to get beyond this. Who are you training, or when are you going to recruit someone into these roles? How much will this cost the business? Are these costs factored into the plan?

Your key staff

Every business with staff has a few key people who are vital to the success of the company. What are you doing to retain and motivate these people? How will you lock them into the business long-term? How will you prevent them from joining your competitors? You need to have good contracts in place, but you also need to be a good leader whom these people believe in and want to work for. This takes practice and hard work. Do everything you can to learn leadership skills.

You also need to ensure that the financial rewards package is adequate. It doesn't always need to beat the competition though. As long as people enjoy working with you and believe in the work they do, the salary is less important, but it can't be too far behind what they could earn elsewhere.

Future development

When you do have a management team and key staff you need to keep developing them. What have you budgeted for training? For books? For training CDs? For seminars and conferences? What about your own training and development?

It's also important to consider what would happen to the business if any of your management team (including you) or your key staff were unable to work for you anymore. They might leave, become ill or fall under a bus. Incidentally, you'll hear the 'fall under a bus' idea a lot when you are pitching for funding in the UK. It's a nicer way of asking what will happen if you or another important person in the business dies. I don't know why that particular mode of transport has been selected to represent your demise. Just be careful when you cross the road!

Funders will be impressed if you have thought of this and put in place some strategies to cope in this event, such as:

1. **Key man insurance**. We discussed this in the last chapter.

2. **Knowledge transfer**. One of the biggest losses when a key member of the team leaves is what is in their head. Ensure that all contact details for clients, etc., are properly recorded in a company owned system, with notes on conversations and any other communication, so that other people can pick up the contact at a later date. It's always good to get people to cover each other's jobs over holidays or during sick leave, that way more people pick up the key knowledge. Who is your stand-in for every single member of the team, and could they do the job?

3. **Succession plans**. Who will step into your shoes if you find yourself in that fateful encounter with a large passenger vehicle? Make sure you get them ready now, and that everyone knows what the chain of command is.

PLANNING

If you have the right opportunity and the right talent on board, then the next step is to have the proper planning in place. This ranges from a proper sales system to financial planning and planning for problems.

Sales planning

Your business plan will include financial forecasts that will provide projections for your sales, but in running your business you need more details in order to stay on track.

You need a sales plan that sets out monthly, or even weekly, targets for how many new customers you will find, how many of these will be converted into sales, what the average sale order value will be and so on. You may choose different measures, but you need to have something against which to track your progress on a regular basis, and you need to look for warning signs. It is important to include contact with potential new customers in your plans, so that you are building up sales for the future. It's all too easy to get dragged into hunting for an extra, quick sale for this month's sales figures, only then to find you have to do the same the next month, and the month after that, because you are not laying the groundwork properly.

Design a process for achieving a sale. For example:

1. Find potential new customer.

2. Research customer to find out need for our products, current supplier, etc.

3. Send a letter of introduction with brochure.

4. Telephone to chat about potential opportunities and arrange a meeting.

5. Have a meeting and find out about customer's needs.

6. Prepare a proposal, send to customer.

7. Telephone customer to get feedback. Negotiate on proposal.

8. Refine the proposal or provide further information. Handle any objections.

9. Take the order.

10. Deliver the order.

11. Follow up to check satisfaction and start work on next order.

At each stage of this process some potential sales will come to a grinding halt, as you find out that they have a three-year exclusive contract with their existing supplier, that they won't have a meeting with you, or that you can't agree suitable terms for a deal. That means that you need to deal with many more customers at step 1 than you expect to get through to step 9. Over time you will learn what this ratio is, and that you, for example, have to find ten potential new customers for every one order you expect to take.

You will also learn what the average order values are likely to be for each customer, and so you will be able to factor this into your planning. Develop this plan, and we will use a summary of it in the business plan in the next chapter. Funders will be impressed!

Cash planning

It will impress funders even further if you have paid careful attention to planning your cash flow. There will be an overview cash flow forecast in your business plan, but for the management of your business you should have a more detailed short-term forecast – and it really helps to let funders see that you do this. We'll assume you will plan cash flow on a week-by-week basis. In that instance you should have a rolling three-month plan. That means that as each week passes you add a further week on to the end of the plan. For the income section, each week you should forecast what sales receipts you expect to clear into your bank account – this means that if you expect to receive a cheque on Thursday, you have to put it into the following week's cash flow to allow time for it to clear. Be pessimistic about income – it's far better to get a pleasant surprise when a payment arrives early or on time than a nasty surprise and a panic when it arrives later than expected.

In expenditure, you'll have certain immovable payments that have to go out in specific weeks – salaries, loan payments, direct debits, etc. After that there will be some expenditure where the week in which it appears can be altered – supplier payments that are made by cheque and so on. You have some flexibility with these, but not a lot if you don't want to risk annoying your suppliers.

Success factors

The business plan, which we will work to develop in Chapter 4, is a large and detailed document, and that makes it difficult to use in the daily running of the company. Funders will be impressed if you are aware of the key things from the plan that everyone's attention should be focused on, and use them to lead your company. These are your success factors.

All success factors

Before we can work out your critical success factors we need to find out what all of the success factors are. Write down a list of everything that needs to happen to make your plans reality:

- What are the key purchasing items and costs to meet or reduce?

- What talent do you need to recruit or develop?

- What product or service developments do you need to make by when?

- When do things need to be launched?

- What parts of the sales plan need to be implemented by when?

- How many new target customers need to be approached by which dates?

- Which sales need to be made by which date?

- Which sales invoices do you need to collect payment on by which date?

- What finance do you need to raise, from where and by when?

- And so on.

This list is very much like a fully extended version of the action plan in the business plan (see Chapter 4). Work with your management team to write down everything that needs to happen.

Critical success factors

Next go through the list and identify the items that, if not done properly or on time, could lead your company into critical problems. These will mainly focus on keeping enough cash in the company through funding, sales and getting invoices paid, but they will also need to include other key events that could seriously damage your business in the short term. Each critical success factor can be a clearly stated heading, with specific actions underneath.

Example – critical success factors:

1. Ensure the business has enough cash
   a) Collect payment on our invoices on time.
   b) Invoice for new sales immediately.
   c) Secure bank overdraft of £50k by June.

2. Generate new sales
   a) Generate £75k of repeat sales a month.
   b) Target ten new customers a month.
   c) Win two new customers a month.

It is important to stick to the absolute possible minimum number of critical success factors in order to focus people's attention on what is really, really important. Look at each one you list – does it justify its position on the critical list, or could it be moved to the important list?

Important success factors

The next level to identify is the action items that won't kill the business (at least in the short term) if they aren't achieved, although they could damage it or store up problems for the future. These could be issues to do with talent, suppliers, product development and so on. Although they won't kill the business next month if they go wrong, they might cause enough damage to your company to prove fatal in the mid to long term.

Example – important success factors:

1. Launch new product by November.

2. Recruit two new sales people by September.

3. Gain positive coverage for new product launch in trade press by end-December.

4. Produce marketing brochure for new product and distribute to existing customers by end-October.

5. Implement customer referral programme by July.

Identifying threats

Remember that funders know things won't go to plan for you, and that they will be relieved if you realize this as well. So demonstrate that you have understood that problems will happen, and that you are doing some work to anticipate them and mitigate against them. There is a tool to help you identify threats, called the PESTEC framework. Simply work through this list and think about what problems could be caused for your business in each area:

1. Political. New laws or regulations might be introduced. These could specifically affect your industry, or relate more generally to your business such as health and safety or data protection regulations. The government's shifting policy may also affect what grants or subsidies are available, or the ability of foreign competitors to enter your market.

2. Economic. Interest rate changes will affect the cost of borrowing, or investments that your company may have. Taxes will affect your profitability and competitiveness. What would happen to your business if there were a slowdown in the housing market, a general slowdown in the economy, or even a recession? What would happen if there was an economic boom? How do currency exchange rates affect your business?

3. Social. Fashions and trends come and go. What's the next big thing? How are public tastes and attitudes changing? What about the social pressures on your target market? Are they working fewer hours, taking more holidays, starting families later, and so on? What does this mean for your business?

4. Technological. Depending on your industry this may be the area you need to watch most closely as things can change so quickly. What will the new technology be for your industry? What will your competitors be using? What new technology will be available to your customers and how will that affect what they want from you? Can you deliver elements of your services over the internet or mobile networks? How can technology help you to become more efficient and competitive?

5. Environmental. This can be environmental in a bigger sense. What will global warming, changing weather, warmer winters, or rainier summers mean for your business? It could also relate to your local environment. What new buildings are planned and how will that affect your business? What other changes might be about to happen in your area?

6. Competitive. This is the key one. Your competitors will be actively working against you, trying to launch products that are better than yours, trying to target your customers and so on. What are they up to now? What are they planning? What are they just thinking about? What trade shows will they be exhibiting at? What advertising campaigns are they running? What press coverage are they getting? Are they recruiting or laying off staff? How are customers reacting to their work? You get the idea – anything you can find out about your competitors helps to build a picture of what they are doing.

Your funders will be aware of this framework, but might use the 'C' to denote 'Cultural'. However, I believe this to be covered by 'Social', and that 'Competitive' is an important area of threats to examine. I'm just explaining that so you can respond to any questions about it!

So, you've now done the work to get your business into shape by focusing on getting your opportunity, talent and planning right. We can now demonstrate this to your potential funders by developing an impressive business plan.

AND FINALLY, YOU

Your business is in shape now, but what about you? We have already seen how the 'talent' in the business is the first thing that funders look at, so how do you measure up? Do you have impressive qualifications, career history, or other experience? Do you already have a great reputation in your industry? Do you have a track record of starting other successful businesses, running other successful businesses – or have you already proved yourself in the way you are running this business? Do you have the key skills that are needed to take the business through this next stage of development? If not, how could you go about learning them?

Funders will want strong signs of your commitment to the business. Would you take a cut in salary? Sell your fancy car? Sell your house and move to a smaller one to release some funds to invest yourself? Will you sign a contract to commit to the business for a certain period or face penalties? Any way that you can demonstrate your commitment to the business will earn you Brownie points from funders.

One way to really deter a funder is for you to expect a high salary and a flashy company car while you are begging them to invest money in your company. They will want to see their money used to develop the company, not your fancy lifestyle. Wait until the profits from the company justify a high salary for you – until then take only modest drawings from the company. For the first couple of years in my first start-up company I took out about £6000 a year, and lived like a student in a shared house. Even once I was on a more normal salary, I would still not take my salary for a month or two if the cash flow was tight. You have to understand that as the entrepreneur the buck stops with you – and therefore be prepared to take responsibility, and the consequences, if sometimes the bucks stop *before* they get to you.

Obviously, some people have other responsibilities in their lives besides their own survival, and if that includes you, you'll need to make sure you can keep the roof over your head and food on the table. A funder won't want you to be worrying about this – they'll want you to have enough money to live reasonably comfortably. They want all your attention to be on the business, but they will also want you to have enough incentive to make the business successful, so it's about striking the right balance.

If you are raising any funding from financial institutions such as banks or leasing companies, they will certainly run a personal credit check on you, as well as on any other business owners or directors, even if your business is a limited company. Your bank will do this simply to open a bank account for you, even if you don't want to borrow any money at all. If you're UK-based it's well worth obtaining a copy of your credit record from each of the three credit reference agencies now, so that you are aware of any potential black marks against your name in advance, giving you time to sort it out.

Each of these agencies must, by law, provide you with a copy of your statutory credit report within ten days of your requesting it. They are allowed to charge a maximum fee of £2. This is a legal requirement on them under the Data Protection Act, in return for being allowed to store so much personal information about people, and to sell that information to financial organizations. However, they will try everything they can to sell you a different version of your credit report for a lot more money. Stand your ground and demand the statutory report for £2.

Equifax credit reference agency:
https://www.econsumer.equifax.co.uk/consumer/uk/gb_
consumerletter.ehtml
Tel: 0870 599 2299
Equifax PLC, Credit File Advice Centre, PO Box 1140, Bradford
BD1 5US
Enclose a cheque for £2 payable to Equifax Plc.

Experian credit reference agency:
http://www.experian.co.uk/consumer/index.html
Tel: 0870 241 6212
CHS Experian, PO Box 8000, Nottingham, NG80 7WF
Enclose a cheque or postal order for £2 payable to Experian Ltd.

CallCredit credit reference agency:
www.callcredit.co.uk
Tel: 0870 060 1414
Consumer Services Team, PO Box 491, Leeds, LS3 1WZ
Enclose a cheque or postal order for £2 payable to Callcredit Plc.

There are equivalent credit agencies in other countries – find out what they are and make sure you do the same if you're based outside Britain.

CHAPTER FOUR
Preparing your plan

Now that you know what funders are looking for, and you have got your business into shape with this in mind, it's time to prepare the business plan to show what you intend to do, and how much finance you need to raise in order to do it.

Your business plan isn't just a document to present to your bank manager or investors, it's a map to direct you as you work, so you should write it as much for your own guidance as for raising money – and you should definitely write it yourself. Funders can always tell when a business plan has been put together by your accountant, and while that means the plan is very professional, they worry about your level of knowledge of the business, and whether the plan really reflects what you can do. They would rather have a plan that is slightly less professional but a lot more 'real'.

So what do you need to put in your plan?

Most people expect a business plan to project forward about two years in detail, with perhaps a further one to three years in summary. However, if you are planning a very big project which will take a substantial amount of investment before reaching profitability or positive cash flow, you will need to forecast forward until these points are reached.

Business plans vary in content and structure depending on your industry and the size of your business now, but here is my suggested structure:

1. **Executive summary**. This is between one and three pages long and simply summarizes the rest of the plan with a couple of paragraphs for each section. The idea is that by reading this

section the reader should understand the business, the opportunity and the headline financial projections. It should also make them want to read the rest of the plan! If this section doesn't press the right buttons it is unlikely that funders will read any further – they are busy people. It's best if you write the rest of the plan first, and then produce a summary at the end of the process.

2. **The company.** Outline your company purpose, some background history, some key past or current financial results and some information about your position in the marketplace and your achievements. It's also worth introducing any investors you already have on board. List your advisers such as accountants, lawyers, bankers, etc. If you have a good non-executive director on your board, or a good mentor if you are at an earlier stage, that will earn you real Brownie points in this section. You should also show the company's registration details, and current shareholding structure if applicable.

3. **The opportunity.** This section explains what it is that you plan to do, why, who for, and why they will buy. It should demonstrate that customers have a need or a want for your product or service, that you have a unique selling point (USP) and a suitable business model.

4. **Customers.** Set out your research into your ideal target customers, and also write about any existing customers you have.

5. **Sales.** Explain the process you plan to use to generate interest and then sales of your services. The more work you have already done on securing sales, the more impressive this section will be.

6. **The team.** This is where you introduce the key talent in the business, including your management team, and any specialists who give you an advantage when it comes to the particular opportunity you are pursuing.

7. **Facilities and resources.** Set out the premises, equipment, IT systems, websites, suppliers, etc., that you have or will need to acquire in order to pursue the opportunity and achieve the plan.

8. **Action plan and risks.** Your action plan is a more detailed list of

what you will do, in what order, and by what date, when you put this plan into action. This is like a big to-do list. You should then set out the critical success factors.

You should also include a brief summary of the main things that could go wrong (see the planning section in the Chapter 3), what you would do if they happened and what you have done already to minimize the impact of the problem..

9. **Financial projections.** In this section you provide a written summary and some tables and graphs to illustrate the key points of the full financial forecasts. Attach the full forecasts at the end of the plan.

10. **Funding plan.** In this section you set out what funding you are looking to raise, how you plan to raise it, what the funders get in return, whether further funding will be required in the future and how the funders will get their exit.

11. **Attachments.** Include a monthly profit forecast for at least the first year, possibly two, and then a summary of the annual profit forecast for another one to three years. You should also include a cash flow forecast for the first year. In many cases, especially when you are seeking bank finance or a large amount of funding, you will also be expected to prepare a balance sheet for your business. If you run an existing business you should attach your most recent full-year accounts. You should also attach a brief CV or one-sided career summary for each member of your management team and for key staff.

Business plans aren't just for companies that are starting up or raising finance, however. It is worth updating your business plan every year where most companies simply do an annual budget. Don't just examine and plan the numbers, examine and plan the whole idea behind the business and its strategy. You may want to involve certain members of your team in this, or even involve all your team members in certain key decisions.

So let's look in more detail at each part of the plan.

THE EXECUTIVE SUMMARY

This is the most important part of your business plan. It is the first thing that funders will read, and if it doesn't persuade them to read the rest of the plan you will have failed. It needs to be a clearly written summary of the contents of the plan as a whole, and it needs to communicate everything that is important in just a couple of pages. But don't be tempted just to write it like a sales brochure for your company. Funders will want to see facts to back up every claim. They will want a professional approach, and may be deterred by your singing your own praises too much. Make it very clear what the opportunity is, why it's an opportunity and how you will take advantage of it.

Things that attract funders in an executive summary:

- Clear, professional writing style in short paragraphs.

- Analytical style with facts and figures to back up your claims.

- A clearly stated opportunity.

- A clearly stated USP – or why you are better than anyone else.

- A summary of the key financial projections.

Things that deter funders in an executive summary:

- Not understanding what it is that your business does or will do – normally because the entrepreneur can't explain it (this is surprisingly common – leave out the jargon and use clear English to avoid it).

- Obviously unrealistic spin and hype – 'Bloggs Motors will become the leading car manufacturer in the world.' They are likely to think that you'll have a tough time against Ford, and dismiss you as a nutter. Plan in bin, end of story.

- Foolish assumptions about what your sales will be. Funders particularly dislike statements such as, 'The UK market for ball-bearings is worth £200m per annum. If we can take just 10 per cent of the market we will have sales of £20m a year.'

- Criticizing your competitors. This is also true throughout the plan, but in particular don't be tempted into it in the executive summary. Show a healthy respect for your competition and you will impress the funders.

- Poor management team or key staff. Be sure to demonstrate any experience and skills that distinguish you.

- Not enough growth potential. This is mainly true for equity investors, as they need to see a high potential for growth in order to make a decent return on their investment. Demonstrate the real potential in your business early on and you will have them hooked.

- Poor spelling and grammar. Again, this is true throughout the whole plan, but doubly important in the executive summary. There is no excuse. Computers highlight errors for you, so correct them. As a last step before sending out the plan get others to check it through for errors.

- Silly fonts and clip art. You are presenting a serious business plan, not entertaining children.

THE COMPANY

In this part of the business plan you will outline what it is that your company does (or will do), what your track record is and other key information about the actual business that is presenting the plan. Include:

- A brief history of the company, showing how it is was formed, how it has developed, key milestones in its growth, key customers, etc.

- Any details of awards you have won or press coverage you have gained (you can include cuttings, etc., in the attachments at the back of the plan).

- Details of the current shareholders and their equity stakes in the business.

- Details of any debt finance currently in the business, what it was used for, whether it is secured on anything, how it is being repaid, etc.

- A summary of key assets in the business: property, machinery, etc.

- Details of your advisers, including accountants, lawyers, bankers, consultants, etc.

- Details of your board structure, including any non-executive directors if you have them.

- Details of your mentor if you are a start-up and you have one.

- A brief overview of recent financial performance if applicable – headline figures from your last two years' annual accounts.

- Any information on how you are placed in your market.

Things that will attract a funder in this section:

- A demonstrable track record of success and growth.

- A good brand name.

- Having a respected non-executive director or two if you are an established business.

- Having a good mentor if you are a start-up.

Things that will deter a funder in this section:

- Lack of a good track record will be a deterrent if you are seeking a large amount of funding.

- A high level of existing debt with no clear resulting achievements.

- Poor financial performance in the past, with no clear reasons. If there are good reasons, then state them – for example, 'We have been investing heavily for two years in developing a ground-breaking new product, and researching export markets.'

THE OPPORTUNITY

This section of the business plan needs to excite the funder. Explain what the opportunity is that you plan to pursue, and explain why it is a great opportunity. You should demonstrate that you have something different – a USP – either in terms of the product or service itself, or in terms of the way you will provide it to your customers. You need to make it very, very clear what this difference is. Set out a summary of who your target customer groups are for this opportunity.

You also need to make it clear that you understand your marketplace. Who currently provides this kind of product or service? You need to analyze who your competitors are for each target customer group. Who do customers buy from already, what are their strengths and weaknesses, what is their USP, what do they charge? How will you provide something better than they do? What can you charge for this product or service? How have you arrived at that decision? What experience do you have in the company that will help you to capitalize on this opportunity?

What will attract funders in this section:

- A clearly explained opportunity that they can understand.

- A genuine need among your target customers.

- A genuine advantage that you have over your competitors in meeting this need for your customers (your USP).

- A clear and sustainable way of earning money from this opportunity.

- Ideas of where the next opportunities for the business may lie.

What will deter funders in this section:

- An unconvincing USP.

- Lack of a clear need or want among target customers.

- Doubt about how to make money from this opportunity.

- Lack of evidence that people will pay for this.

- Brash over-confidence that is not backed up by research.

CUSTOMERS

Set out your definitions for your target customer types, along with their brief fictional descriptions. Then show how you conducted research on each type of customer, and what you found. Show where the need is and what the buying motivations are. Set out how many customers are available to target in each group according to your research. If possible include quotations from real or potential customers – this can help a lot. This is the place to show off if you have already managed to get customers to place an order, or give a commitment to order.

What will attract funders in this section:

- Having sales or commitments to order. You will go straight to the top of the class!

- Being focused on who your target customers are.

- Knowing a lot about your target customers.

What will deter funders in this section:

- Statements like, 'We expect to capture 10 per cent of the market,' with little or no evidence of knowledge about how you will win customers.

- Little or no research into potential customers.

- No clear finding that your customers really need what you are offering

SALES

You have identified your target customers, and in Chapter 3 you developed a sales plan to help you understand the stages involved in winning orders, and the number of potential customers you need to put through each stage. Explain that process in this section of the business plan, setting out what each stage will involve. How will you find potential customers? Will you have already made them aware of your company through advertising and PR? Will they be approaching you? Will you be cold-calling them? How will you research each customer? How will you approach them? How will you prepare the proposal? And so on.

In this section you should give the funders confidence that you know exactly what to do in order to win the business of your target customers.

What will attract funders:

- The fact that a clear sales plan exists at all.
- The fact that you have carefully thought about each stage of the sales process.

What will deter funders:

- A lack of certainty about how to turn potential customers into sales.
- Unrealistic expectations of how many prospects will turn into sales.
- Not being prepared for likely objections from potential customers.
- Not having a convincing sales pitch.

THE TEAM

In this section of the plan you can give brief biographies of your management team and your key staff. Keep it relevant though – what experience, contacts, training and skills do they have that are going to help you achieve this plan? What staff will you need to recruit over the course of the plan? How will you find them? How will you train them? How will you reward them – with what salary, any shares, bonuses, etc.? How does this compare with the market rates?

What skills gaps do you have in the company and how do you plan to fill them? By recruiting? By using advisers? If you plan to raise funding from business angels, you may specifically set out to find an angel who can help you fill this skills gap – if that's the case, make it clear. If you are raising funds from venture capital firms, they have extensive contacts books and can help you fill high-level skills gaps in your company as part of their investment.

What will attract funders:

- Having people with experience and contacts in your market.

- Having a clear and realistic plan for recruitment and training.

- A management team prepared to take a low salary in the early stages of a business (if you are a start-up).

What will deter funders:

- A large proportion of their investment going on fancy salaries for the management team. It happens quite often that a loss-making business needs to raise, for example, £100k, but the owner demands that they should be able to take £50k a year in salary. Funders will want to see you share the risk until your business profits can justify a higher salary.

- No clear strategy for recruitment as the business grows.

- Lack of clear experience or skills in key areas for the business.

- Key members of staff not locked into the business.

FACILITIES AND RESOURCES

In this part of the plan you set out the other things you will need to have in place to help the talent do their job and provide your customers with your products and services. This may be office space, warehouse space, retail space or other property. It may be computers, machinery or other technology. Think carefully about what your team needs, what you have already and therefore what you need to buy. But try to keep the costs down.

You are also likely to need suppliers to provide raw materials, services or specialist expertise. Which suppliers will you choose, what will they charge, and how will you manage them? What backup will you have if they fail to deliver or go out of business? And think about what other resources you may need. Advertising design? PR? Packaging design? Vehicles? The list could be endless. Be sure you cover everything – what it will cost, when you need it and how you will fund it.

What will attract funders:

- A frugal management team which have begged, borrowed and not-quite-stolen the resources to run the business. Get the best value possible, while retaining quality. Use your brains instead of a big budget.

- Careful research and planning for suitable suppliers and backup options.

What will deter funders:

- A management team which have splashed out vast sums of money to get big flashy offices in the best location possible, get the best cars, buy brand new machinery all at top rate and so on.

- No close working relationships or contacts with key suppliers that are vital to your business.

Action plan and risks

In the action plan you set out the key things you are going to do to make this plan a reality once you have raised the funding. You can also show the Success Factors that you have identified (see page 53), and how you will monitor them.

You should also show that you have thought about and identified the main risks to the business, and explain how you are going to protect against them (see page 33 and page 55).

FINANCIAL PROJECTIONS

Now that you have written about what you intend to do in your business, it is time to start putting some numbers to your plans. That is the right way round to do it – don't be tempted to start with the numbers and then try to concoct a written plan around that. I've included some examples of what your financial forecasts should look like on the following pages, as well as describing them below.

You may well already have experience in making and presenting financial projections, but in case you are a seed or start-up business, I'm going to set it out step by step.

Early-stage, growth or turnaround business entrepreneurs can really benefit from reading *The Definitive Business Plan* by Richard Stutely, which offers much more detail about creating financial projections. (For further details about this book, see p. xii.)

Sales forecast

Before you get on to the more in-depth financial forecasts, you need to work out how much you can sell in each month in your first year.

To do this, start a spreadsheet or a piece of paper with the columns for each of the first 12 months of your business, and then the following rows:

Product 1 Unit price
Product 1 Unit sales
PRODUCT 1 SALES VALUE

Product 2 Unit price
Product 2 Unit sales
PRODUCT 2 SALES VALUE

And so on. You can do the same with services, or billable hours. Replace product numbers with product names. Put the price in all the columns. Now for the forecasting. In the unit sales row, put in each month the number of units or hours that you think you can sell of that product or service. You can estimate the number of units you will sell in a month by starting with thinking about how many you could sell in a day.

If you are a seed or start-up business, or you are an existing business launching new products or services or entering new markets, then forecasting your financial incomings and outgoings is incredibly difficult, and some of the numbers are, frankly, going to be guesses. That's all right, but you have to have some reasoning to back these guesses.

Profit forecast

Your business plan should include a profit forecast (accountants usually call this a profit and loss forecast, but let's think positively!).

Most start-up businesses, or other businesses investing in growth or turnaround, incur losses in the early phase of the plan which can last months or years depending on the type of business. The most important thing is to achieve a manageable cash flow.

A profit forecast shows the income and expenditure in the business as it is incurred – recorded at the point at which the invoice is received or sent for costs or sales respectively. The forecast includes the following sections down the left hand side of the page.

SALES

We've started by doing a separate forecast for sales, above, and that makes this section much easier. In this part of the profit forecast you summarize the value of that forecast. It's best to break this section down a bit with a line for each product type – but you don't need to go as far as a line for every single product! For example, if you were an IT business you would have a line each for 'Hardware sales', 'Software sales', 'Support contracts', 'Installation fees'. Under all these put a line for 'TOTAL SALES'.

COST OF SALES

These are any costs that you incur in order to fulfil a sale. They include the cost of any products that you would buy in. So, in the example of our IT company, if they planned to sell a network of 20 computers, they would have costs of sale that include buying in 20 computers, a server, software and network cables from their suppliers at trade prices. Again, summarize these by type of product or service rather than listing every possible item, and then put a total underneath this section.

CONTRIBUTION

This is often referred to by accountants as 'gross profit', but I don't like to start bandying the 'P' word around just yet – because there are plenty of costs still to come! What this section shows is the contribution your sales are making to the overheads and profits of the business. In other words, the income that is left once the cost of sales has been accounted for. So, to calculate this figure for each month on your plan, subtract the total cost of sales from the total sales.

OVERHEADS

In this section you list all the costs of the business that have to be paid regardless of whether you make any sales. This section will include lines for: rent, salaries, employers' tax/NI, expenses, telephone, light/heat/power, stationery/postage, etc.

You may also need to include depreciation on any capital expenditure. (This is the purchase of machinery, IT or other high-value items that you will use over a number of years. Depreciation means that if a computer cost £900 and will last you three years, you might only show the cost of £300 in each of those three years on your profit forecast instead of taking the full cost of £900 in the first year.) It should be noted that the Inland Revenue have rules on the rates of depreciation allowed for computing taxable profits. You do not have to use the same rates in your management accounts but it makes things simpler.

Once you have calculated all these figures you need to total up all your overheads at the bottom.

PROFIT BEFORE INTEREST AND TAX (PBIT)

This single line simply shows the result of subtracting your overheads from your contribution. Hopefully it's positive!

INTEREST

Here you show the interest that you will be charged on any bank loans, overdrafts, etc., and any interest that you will receive from investments.

PROFIT BEFORE TAX

This is generally the final line on profit forecasts – and you've probably guessed that it simply shows your PBIT minus the total interest.

A bank or investor may also require a balance sheet as part of your plans. This shows the assets and liabilities of the business at a fixed point in time. In a forecast this might show the balance sheet at the end of each month in the plan. Your bookkeeper or accountant can help with the preparation of a balance sheet.

The moment of truth

Now that you have a forecast, there are some important calculations to make to see if it works!

Your break-even point for the year

This is the amount of sales required to make a profit in your business in the 12 months of this forecast. To calculate it, look at the profit forecast and do the following calculations:

1. Add up all your monthly total sales to get a figure for the year. Call this figure A.

2. Add up all your total cost of sales to get a figure for the year. Call this figure B.

3. Add up all your total overheads to get a figure for the year. Call this figure C.

4. The first calculation is A minus B to get the total contribution (gross profit) for the year. Call this figure D.

5. Next calculate this as a percentage of sales: D divided by A, then multiplied by 100. Call this figure E.

6. Finally calculate your break-even point: C divided by E, then multiplied by 100.

7. The result is the amount of sales you need to make in order to make a profit – your break-even point.

Do your total sales pass this point during the year? If not, how far away from your break-even point are you over the year – that is how does the break-even point compare with your total sales (figure A) for the whole year? Is there a way you could realistically:

1. Increase your sales over the year?

2. Reduce your cost of sales over the year?

3. Reduce your overheads over the year?

You can also continue forecasting further into the future until you can show at least a year of continued profitability at the end of your forecast. You should continue forecasting on a monthly basis until your break-even point is reached, but after that you can simply provide an annual summary forecast. As a rule of thumb, it's usual to provide monthly forecasts for the first two years, and then annual summaries beyond that extending to a total of three to five years.

Is it ever going to be possible to pass your break-even point? If not, it's time to think seriously about your business model. You're either not selling enough, not charging enough, or your costs are too high. If you can't fix these you may have to look at another idea. Time for a conversation with your mentor or your accountant! If it is going to take a long time (more than six to twelve months) for your sales to reach a break-even point, this may also indicate a problem in your forecast. Talk to your mentor or accountant. This may be acceptable if yours is a very new type of product or service and it's going to take a while to test, educate and grow the market – but you'll need to have funding for your business in the meantime.

Your monthly break-even point

If you do break even in your first six months or so, and you are happy with your forecast, you can continue by calculating your monthly break-even point. This is simply the break-even point you calculated above, divided by 12. It tells you how much you must sell every month in order to break even. This is an important business management figure, and funders will want to see that you have done this calculation.

You now know when you will be able to make your business profitable, and how much profit you can make. Profitability is good, but the most important part of planning and running your business is forecasting and managing the flow of cash in and out of the business.

Profit is, of course, important in planning your business success, but it becomes irrelevant if you run out of cash. Cash is the fuel for your business – if you run out of it you come crashing down to earth. To avoid this you need to plan your cash flow carefully.

Cash flow forecast

Your cash flow forecast is divided into the following sections: income, expenditure and financing.

Under the income heading you put all your sales income, but also income from any equipment or other assets you plan to sell, at the time you expect to receive the cash.

Under the expenditure heading you put all the costs that you have to pay out, including to suppliers for the goods you bought under the cost of sales in the profit forecast as well as the costs in the overheads section. Don't include non-cash items such as depreciation. You should add in the full costs of any capital expenditure you expect to make. Put these in at the point at which you expect to have to pay the cash out.

Under the financing heading you list any cash that your business receives or pays out in relation to the funding of the company. So this might include investment into the company by shareholders, receiving a bank loan, repayments on a bank loan, etc. Also include a separate line showing payments of interest on financing. Show any payments out as negative amounts.

Following these three sections you have a three-line summary:

Opening balance. This is the amount of cash that you have at the start of the month.

Cash flow. This is the total of income, minus expenditure, plus financing. It will be a positive number if cash flows into your business during the month, or a negative number if cash flows out of the company in the period.

Closing balance. This is the opening balance plus the cash flow. This amount is then carried forward to be the next month's opening balance.

If there are months where the closing balance is negative this indicates that you need to find extra financing for your business by making more sales in that period, collecting money earlier, increasing prices, paying suppliers later by arrangement, or arranging an overdraft with your bank. Alternatively you can seek to reduce or delay expenditure.

The main difference between your cash flow forecast and your profit forecast is that figures are not recorded at the point of invoice, but at the point of payment. That means you forecast sales income into the plan at the point at which the money will actually clear into your bank account and be available to spend, while you forecast expenditure at the point at which you will have to pay for items.

There are a few other key differences:

1. Generally, if you are registered for VAT, your profit forecast won't include VAT because you simply collect it from your customers and pay it to HMRC minus the VAT you are reclaiming, so it doesn't affect your profits. It does affect your cash flow, however, so you include VAT on any sales amounts and any purchases, and you have a line in your forecast showing the VAT that you are due to pay to (or reclaim from) HMRC.

2. Do not include depreciation in your cash flow forecast, but do include the actual cost of any capital expenditure you plan to make.

How does the cash flow look?

During the start-up phase or at a time of high investment in a growing business, it is to be expected that you will have some negative figures in the first half of your cash flow forecast. The key is, what is the largest negative figure? This is how much finance you need to get into the business. Does it make your eyes water? If so, get some advice from your accountant or mentor. If the figures are mostly negative throughout your cash flow, there is a problem with your business model, and you need to review the number of sales you plan to make, what costs you have and other factors. Your accountant and mentor can advise you. Again though, the exception to this is if you are working long-term to build quite a large business, or a product or service that is new and different, for which it will take time to establish a market. You just have to be sure you can get the funding.

THE FUNDING PLAN

The final section in your plan is where you set out exactly how much money you intend to raise, and how you intend to raise it. This is to show your funders exactly what you are asking for, and what they will get in return. You can only really write this section of the plan after you have been through the next few chapters and identified how best to raise funding, so return to this later, but do read it now so that you know what to be thinking about while we look at funding types.

In this section, begin by explaining how much funding you need to raise in total, bearing in mind that it is best to raise a little more than your plan shows that you absolutely must have, as things never go to plan and it will be much harder to raise more funds later if things haven't worked – so get a bit of breathing space now! Then you need to explain how this will be broken down: how much funding will you raise in which way? For example, £20k equity investment, £20k bank loan, £10k director's own investment.

If you are raising equity investment, set out how many shares you plan to sell to raise that amount of money, and what that values the business at. For example, if you are selling 20 shares priced at £1000 each, and you will have 80 shares, then you are valuing the business at £100,000 – and you are offering them a 20 per cent share in the business for £20,000. Explain your justification for this valuation of your business, highlighting future profits. If you are raising debt finance, specify how much you expect to receive in the form of a loan, and how much in the form of an overdraft. What security can you offer? If it's a loan and you can't provide security, do you plan to apply under the government's loan guarantee scheme? The same applies for other sources of finance. List how much you plan to raise from that source, what you will give in return and any other relevant information. Finally, set out when and how you expect equity investors to be able to exit the business and what return they will make on their investment.

REVIEWING THE PLAN

Make sure that your plan flows, is easy to read, is well presented – simple and clear rather than flashy – and that it makes sense. Read it through thoroughly and ask yourself these questions, pretending that you are a bank manager who knows nothing about the business except what is in this plan:

1. Do I understand what this business will do?

2. Is it clear why this business will do it better than anyone else?

3. Is it clear that people want to pay for what this business does?

4. Who will the first customers be?

5. Do the management understand the industry and the marketplace?

6. Do the management appreciate the challenges ahead, and have they prepared for them?

7. How much finance is going to be needed, and where will it come from?

8. Is the business financially viable? Can it make good profits?

9. Can the business survive on the cash it will have available?

You will probably want to do some more work on the plan after this exercise, in order to be certain that all these questions are clearly answered.

5

CHAPTER FIVE
Types of funding

In this chapter we will look at all the main sources of funding for small businesses at all stages. Typically, entrepreneurs will use a number of different types of funding in starting or growing their business, and I really encourage you to put together a blend of different types that suits your business and your situation.

The types of funding we will look at are:

a) Sales

b) Equity

c) Debt

d) Asset finance

e) Business support

f) Blagging.

A. SALES

There are four ways of using sales to fund your business.

First, you can improve your cash flow by making a greater number of more profitable sales through increasing your prices, getting paid in advance or up-selling – without having to increase your overheads. Second, if you are just starting a business, you could begin by offering a simpler product or service to start with, and use the money earned from this to invest in your main business. Third, finance companies will lend to you based on your sales invoices, and this can improve your cash flow. Finally, you can sell something different from your main product to help you finance that main product.

Funding your business through sales

Many entrepreneurs overlook sales as a potential source of funding for their business, but it is simply the best possible way to generate cash because you don't have to give equity in return, you don't have to pay interest on it and you don't have to pay it back! Seems obvious doesn't it?

Here are the main ways to generate cash from your sales.

Increase your prices

You will have already looked at this in the section on getting your business into shape ready for investment. If you are able to increase your prices, then any extra money raised is pure profit and is immediately available for investing in your business.

Take payment in advance

If you can improve your cash flow you can reduce or remove the need to rely on external sources of funding. The best way to improve cash flow is to take payment for at least some of each sale in advance.

If you're dealing with large companies, and have a good relationship with them, then you will be surprised how many will be perfectly happy to pay substantial amounts of your fees in advance of your doing the work or delivering the goods – particularly if it's coming up to the end of their financial year and they have some budget to use up! Even smaller businesses (with good cash flow) can be persuaded to pay upfront if they can get a small discount. A discount of as little as 2 per cent for paying an invoice 30 days earlier than they would otherwise need to makes a lot of sense to them, as that is more than they could earn in interest on the money if they left it in their bank account for the same period.

You could also look at putting staged payments into your standard terms and conditions – with payments made at key stages. For example:

- 50 per cent on order, 50 per cent on completion.

- 25 per cent on order, 25 per cent at milestone 1, 25 per cent at milestone 2, 25 per cent on completion.

Even if you can't negotiate a substantial payment in advance you can normally agree that the customer will pay some kind of deposit – businesses and consumers alike are used to this.

Up-sell

A good way of generating extra cash from your existing sales to clients is to sell them additional, complementary products or services that go with what they already buy from you.

Complementary services could be:

- consultancy;

- installation;

- training (on how to use what you've just sold them);

- insurance (sourced from a specialist insurer);

- an annual service contract, giving them a guaranteed response time;

- an extended warranty. (Have you ever tried buying anything in the big-name electrical goods stores? Have they tried to sell you an extended warranty? That's because they make more money on the warranty than they do on the product you're buying!)

Some examples of complementary products are:

- You've just sold a new car to a customer, so up-sell them a car safety pack with a first aid kit, fire extinguisher, spare oil, spare coolant, etc.

- You've just sold your services as an accountant to a new client, so up-sell them to a 'business support pack' that includes useful books and CDs.

Up-selling can be a very effective way of generating extra sales, because the hardest part of selling is getting the very first buying decision – after that it is much easier to sell new things to the same client because the relationship and the trust are there. It's the equivalent of supermarkets putting sweets at the checkout – you're buying something anyway, so what's the difference in just adding in a chocolate bar? Customers are receptive to buying new things while they are in the process of a purchase.

Use this to give them something that they will find useful, or that will give them pleasure, and to generate more cash for your business.

Agree a longer-term contract

If a customer likes what you do for them, and they want to support your business, they may agree to be tied into a longer-term contract to give you the security of knowing you have a guaranteed income with which to fund your business. The contract could set out a schedule for when payments will be made. This will also reassure any other investors and greatly help in persuading them to invest.

Start with a smaller opportunity

This is a technique that can be used by businesses at the seed or start-up stages which need to raise the money to produce their main product. It involves coming up with a product or service that you can produce very cheaply initially, but which can earn you money to invest in launching your main business.

For example, an entrepreneur who wants to raise the money to develop and launch a hi-tech web-based business could initially begin by designing websites for local businesses. The costs are low – just the founder's time and the use of their computers – but the price they can charge the customer is relatively high. If they were to do this for six months or a year they could raise quite a bit of money to put towards starting their main business – money that will help to prise investment out of other people. An additional advantage is that they will have learned a lot about the web industry and what's involved in running a business, including vital sales skills, which will also be a tick in a box for other investors.

Some entrepreneurs worry that if they don't launch their main business straight away then the opportunity will pass them by, or someone else will get there first. In reality, good opportunities are the ones that are here to stay, and the first to market generally goes bust!

Invoice finance

This is a form of financing offered by the high street banks and a number of specialist finance companies. In essence they buy your invoices from you, giving you up to 85 per cent of the value of the invoice as soon as you send it to your customer, and then paying the rest (minus their fee) when the customer pays the invoice. There are two levels of service – factoring and invoice discounting.

Factoring

This is the full service package in which the provider takes over the relationship with the customer (in relation to payment) from the point of invoice. They send statements, call the customer and generally do whatever it takes to get the customer to pay. This can be a useful service and, if carried out professionally, can be effective without affecting your relationship with the customer. It does mean, however, that there is a vital link with the customer that you are not in control of – you have no idea what the factor's staff are saying to your valuable clients, how motivated they are, how well recruited they are, what impression they are giving of your company, or how that will impact on future sales.

You can expect to pay a finance fee of between 1 per cent and 3 per cent over bank base rate of the amount advanced at any time, plus a service fee of between 0.5 per cent and 3 per cent of your turnover.

Invoice discounting

This is simply a financing service – you are still responsible for collecting the money from your customers, but in other respects it is the same as factoring. The service can be 'disclosed', in which case your invoices will carry a notification that you are using an invoice finance company, or 'confidential' in which case the arrangement will be private.

Again you can expect to pay a finance fee of between 1 per cent and 3 per cent over bank base rate, but the service fee is less than for factoring (because there is less of a service!) at between 0.1 per cent and 1 per cent of your turnover. The finance company will want to be sure that you have proper credit control procedures in place. For more information on invoice finance, visit: www.factors.org.uk

B. EQUITY

Raising funds through selling equity in a business is the route taken by most of the highly successful entrepreneurs, the ones you read about in the papers. It's a great way to fund the kind of high-risk, high-return business that becomes a well-known name. Business angels and venture capitalists all exist simply to invest in promising businesses in this way. But equity funding is available to smaller companies too – you could offer shares to friends and family, and some business angels are willing to look at small investments too, particularly if they are local to you, or have experience in your industry.

Private and public limited companies

Taking on equity investment requires your business to be incorporated as a company limited by shares – the only form of business that has equity available to sell. A private limited company can sell shares to private investors or individuals who are known to it – but can't publicly promote an offer for shares. This is a move to protect members of the public without investment experience from high risks. This type of company is what is generally just referred to as a limited company, and is the most common form. If you want to offer your shares for sale to the general public you need to incorporate as a public limited company – a PLC.

A start-up or early-stage business is most likely to incorporate as a private limited company, while a fast-growth or well-established business may choose the public limited company route – often after having been a private limited company for some years.

Case study

Two friends of mine, John Barnes and Richard Richardson, had bought a fish and chip restaurant in Leeds called Harry Ramsden's, which they wanted to turn into the national brand for fish and chips – the equivalent of what KFC did for chicken (John had been the UK Managing Director of KFC) and Pizza Hut had done for pizza. To get the funds to do this they had originally raised funding from a US bank and investment from a selection of private shareholders. After just one year, however, the bank had a change of strategy and decided they wanted their money back. John and Richard took the unheard-of step of going public with a business that owned just one restaurant. They floated their business on the then 'Third Market', now called 'AIM'. But while it was conventional then to sell all the shares in public companies to large investors, such as pension funds, John and Richard sold most of the shares to members of the public in Yorkshire who knew about the existing restaurant and knew it produced the best fish and chips in the world – and therefore that it was a great business idea to make it a national operation. The public offering was a huge success, with 4000 people buying shares – and giving Harry Ramsden's the funding to open restaurants across the country.

The advantages of equity funding for you are:

1. It doesn't saddle your business with large debts that you have to pay back (with interest) regardless of how well your company is doing.

2. Investors often bring skills, experience, contacts and advice as well as their money.

3. The investors are rewarded only for the success of your business.

4. Having some equity investment in your company can leverage funds from other sources, such as banks, who will often be happy to provide a matching loan, and perhaps even to give a better interest rate to reflect the reduced level of risk.

5. Having an obligation to report on the progress of your business to outside investors can bring great discipline to you and your management team.

The disadvantages for you are:

1. It is like a marriage. Having an equity investor is a long-term relationship. You have to consider whether you can work with them for years to come. Do you both have the same vision and goals for the business?

2. Most investors will want to exit their investment at some point in the future. This may mean that they sell their shares to someone else, or that they push you to sell the business as a whole.

3. If an investor has a large proportion of the shares in the business they could force you out, or sideline you, if they don't approve of the way you are running the business.

4. It can take some time, and a lot of effort, to raise money through equity investment.

5. Someone else will own part of the business, meaning that it's not all yours any more. This can be a difficult psychological barrier for some entrepreneurs.

6. In the long term it can be an expensive way of funding your business, as equity investors want to make very high returns on their money – earning significantly more from investing in you than leaving the money sitting in a savings account. But then you're a lot more risky so that's only fair.

C. DEBT

Interest on debt finance is normally set in relation to 'base rate'. This is the base rate of the bank, or other lender, that you are dealing with, and is usually the same as the base rate of the Bank of England. Debt finance is generally relatively easy to access, and the deals are straightforward to negotiate. If you have a good team, a good opportunity and security to offer on the debt then you are pretty certain to be able to get the finance you need.

Overdraft

This is a form of short-term finance suitable for funding your working capital. It is an expensive way to borrow money. Many entrepreneurs arrange overdraft facilities as a potential emergency fund even though their plan shows that they do not need an overdraft. The big drawback with overdrafts (apart from cost) is that the bank can withdraw them at any time. They will do this if they get the slightest hint of trouble from your company – and suddenly you will find that you have to repay your overdraft. This can send a lot of companies under.

Do not rely on an overdraft as a major source of funding the expansion of your business, it is not the right tool – but it can be ideal for smoothing out your cash flow as you grow. Overdrafts are available from the high street banks.

Overdraft interest rates can be as high as 7 per cent over base rate (but do haggle!). There will also be a fee for arranging an overdraft. The overdraft will be agreed for a set period and a set maximum amount, and if you need to extend either of these then there will be another negotiation and – you've guessed it – another arrangement fee. So negotiate the agreed period to be as long as possible and the maximum amount to be more than sufficient for your needs for some time to come.

Loan

A loan involves borrowing a lump sum of money from a lender, and then repaying it over a set period of time, plus interest at an agreed rate, which can be fixed or variable. With a fixed interest rate you agree a set percentage rate for the whole term of the loan, for example 7.5 per cent. If the base rate then goes up you've probably got a good deal, but if it goes down then you're paying over the odds. A variable rate of interest will be set at a fixed percentage above the bank's base rate, typically between 2.5

per cent and 4 per cent above base rate. This will then change from month to month.

Most of the interest on a loan is paid in the early years of repayments, so take a view on what you think is going to happen in that period to decide whether to opt for fixed or variable interest. Also, remember that the interest rate is negotiable. Haggle as hard as you can! You should also read the agreement for any loan and negotiate on the other key terms (more about negotiation on finance terms later, see p. 194).

When it comes to the term of the loan you need to do your financial planning carefully. The longer you have the loan for, the more you will pay in interest, but if you agree to a shorter term you will have larger monthly repayments – and you will still have to make these repayments even if you have a cash flow problem in a particular month. If you can, it's best to agree a long term for the loan, but with no penalty for repaying the loan early.

Most entrepreneurs who need a loan go straight to their high street bank, but there are much better deals available elsewhere. Building societies, smaller banks, foreign banks and specialist business finance companies are all making the market very competitive. Your accountant may be able to help you, or do a search on the web.

But do make sure you read the small print.

One way a lender may try to catch you out is by insisting that you take out their payment protection insurance. This is rarely a good deal from the lender, and if they insist on your having it, you should insist on shopping around through an insurance broker – or take your business elsewhere.

A loan may also be available to you from friends, family or other business contacts. This can be low or even zero interest, and is well worth taking if the right agreements are in place and you can be sure that they won't suffer if your business runs into problems and is unable to repay them. More on that later.

Trade credit

The most common form of debt finance in business is to ask for trade credit terms from your suppliers. This means that you can take delivery of the products or services and pay for them 30, 60 or sometimes even 90 days later. Suppliers will often start new customers off on very short credit terms, but you should regularly try to negotiate for better terms. This can greatly improve the cash flow in your business, and it's a very cheap, sometimes free, form of finance.

Credit finance

You can have a business credit card, and use this for making purchases in your company – giving you a period of credit on items where you can't get credit terms from the suppliers. These cards work just like personal credit cards, and you get an interest free period of up to 56 days. Interest is then charged if you don't settle your balance in full after a set period following each statement (usually 25 days). Some banks charge an annual fee for business credit cards.

There are also business charge cards, which are like credit cards except you have to pay off the balance in full each month, usually within seven days of receiving the statement. There is usually an annual fee to pay, plus a charge per transaction.

Business credit or charge cards are generally only available from the main banks, but you don't have to get your card from the same bank you have your current account with – shop around. When applying for one, be sure to ask whether it is a credit or a charge card, as both look exactly the same and have generic names such as 'business card'.

D. ASSET FINANCE

In setting up or growing your business you are likely to need to purchase assets such as property, machinery or vehicles. In my view it's crazy to call these things assets as they are not generating sales income for you directly – they are costs! But the finance industry refers to them as assets (because they are solid, expensive things that they can take away from you if your business fails), so that's how we must refer to them. There are various special forms of finance to buy these assets, and they are secured upon the assets themselves.

Commercial mortgage

A commercial mortgage will allow you to borrow up to 80 per cent of the value of the property, meaning that you have to make a deposit of at least 20 per cent, financed through other means. The loan is then secured on the property. It can be used to buy a property, or if you already have a property you may be able to take a mortgage out to provide other funding for the business. A commercial mortgage term is usually for up to 25 years, but some banks are now offering 30-year terms.

To help your cash flow some lenders will allow you a capital repayment holiday, meaning that you only have to make interest payments for an initial period, which in some cases can be up to two years. The agreement may also allow you to defer a certain number of repayments per year, or over the term. Obviously, both of these mean you will be paying more interest in the long term!

Many entrepreneurs forget that the actual price of the property is only part of the cost. You need also to factor in lawyers' fees, surveyors' fees, agents' fees, stamp duty, VAT, search fees and the cost of any refitting or other alterations to get the property into shape for your use (or to comply with health and safety, environmental or disability legislation).

In addition, you can generally expect to pay a 1 per cent arrangement fee, and interest of between 1 per cent and 2.5 per cent over the bank's base rate if you are considered a good credit risk. Companies with a poor track record or a bad credit rating can expect to pay interest of between 2.5 per cent and 5.5 per cent over base rate. You must also beware of early settlement charges that may be hidden in the small print. This can be a major issue if you want to pay down the debt early, or re-mortgage.

Leasing

Leasing (known in full as 'finance leasing') is like renting an asset. You pay regular instalment payments, for a fixed period, to the finance company who has bought the asset on your behalf. In many cases this works out to be better for your cash flow, and (depending on the kind of asset and the agreement you reach with the finance company) the payments may include all repair and maintenance costs. But you will end up paying more for the assets in the end. There are some tax benefits, however, as you can deduct the costs of the lease from your taxable income and you can reclaim the VAT on your payments.

With leasing be careful to select the right period for the lease. Computer equipment, for example, can become outdated in two or three years, other assets might have a useful life of five years, so you need to tailor the lease to suit the estimated lifespan of the asset.

When you start a lease you will pay an administration fee, and an initial payment. This initial payment will usually be calculated as a certain multiple of the regular repayment amount. All the costs of the asset, and the finance interest and charges, will be covered in the agreed period. At the end of the agreed period you can continue to lease the asset for a token amount, or you can give it back to the finance company and start a new lease on a newer replacement item. At no point do you own the asset, so you can't sell it or use it as security.

Operating lease

This is a slight variation on a finance lease, the only difference being that the repayments you make don't cover the full cost of the asset, only the amount between the original cost and what it is likely to be able to be sold for at the end of the lease term (the 'residual value').

Hire purchase (HP)

This allows you to pay for an asset over a set period of time, in agreed regular instalments. It's good for your cash flow because you can spread the payments over a couple of years. You don't legally own the asset until you have made all the payments, but it will be treated as yours for tax purposes, meaning that you may be able to claim 'capital allowances', which allows you to offset some of the costs against your profits. As with leasing it is best to tailor the period over which you will make the payments to the estimated useful life of the asset.

At the start you will pay a deposit of between 10 per cent and 20 per cent to the finance company, an administration fee of between £100 and £200, and the full amount of VAT on the entire purchase. You should then be able to reclaim the VAT if your business is VAT registered. After that you pay the rest of the price of the asset, plus interest, in regular instalments over an agreed period. The interest can be fixed or variable, and will be agreed at the start. At the end of this period you can take ownership of the asset by paying a small 'option to purchase' fee.

Hire

If you don't need to have permanent access to a particular piece of equipment, consider hiring it when you need it. You can rent vehicles, machinery, tools and all sorts of specialist equipment. You can even rent offices by the hour if you need to – so an expanding business doesn't need to open an office in London, you can just rent one there when you need it for meetings, etc. This can reduce costs if your use is infrequent, not just because you don't actually have to buy the thing, but also because you don't have to repair it or have it serviced. It is entirely the responsibility of the hire company.

It's also much easier to hire things than it is to obtain finance for leasing or purchase. Most of us have experienced how easy it is to hire a car – it's just the same as this.

Again, you can deduct your payments for hiring equipment from your taxable income.

Refinancing using existing assets

If you are a growing company or are trying to turn your business around then you may have assets in the business that you own outright, and you could refinance these to release cash into the business.

Sales and leaseback

You may have read a lot about this in the business press as many big companies are doing it with their buildings and other high-value assets at the moment. This is just like a normal leasing arrangement, the difference being that you are the vendor of the asset as well as the lessee. You invoice the finance company for the value of the asset (at the lower of the value of the item on your accounts or the current market value), and then the finance company leases it back to you. You pay a deposit, followed by regular repayments.

Chattel mortgage

This is generally only available in England, and allows you to offer an asset as security to a finance company. The finance company then lends you money secured on this asset. A charge is registered over the assets in the same way as for a mortgage on property.

E. BUSINESS SUPPORT

Grants

Local authorities, government agencies and some charitable trusts offer grants to small businesses. Each available grant tends to be very focused on supporting one type of business. The focus could be any one, or a combination, of the following:

1. A particular geographic area.

2. A particular type of business – e.g. technology, manufacturing.

3. A particular type of entrepreneur – young people, the unemployed, graduates, ethnic minorities, women, short people (my invention) or other specific categories.

4. A particular type of expenditure – creating jobs, buying machinery, building a website, producing a sales brochure.

Often the grant will be to match other expenditure, so the grant might cover between 10 per cent and 75 per cent of the project cost, with you having to fund the rest from other sources.

The great thing about grants is that you don't have to pay them back, and you don't have to pay any interest – it's free money! But wait, there are some catches:

1. The application process is usually a bureaucratic nightmare, administered by people who have no idea about running a business. There will be long, complicated forms to fill out, lots of other documents to provide, endless meetings and innumerable phone calls chasing people up when you have heard nothing for weeks.

2. It will take a very long time to complete the process – often months longer than you think.

3. Some grant schemes are awarded at set times of the year. Murphy's Law says you find out about the perfect grant in May, but the deadline for applications is once a year in April.

4. Most grant schemes don't allow you to have started work on the project they are intended to fund before you have been given the money. One sweet manufacturer I know of urgently needed a piece of machinery to be able to accept a big new order from a major supermarket chain. She needed help to afford the machine and found a local authority grant that would fund 50 per cent of the cost – however, the process would take at least six months and she wasn't allowed even to place the order for the machine until the whole process was complete. Essentially this grant was worthless to her.

So, do research what grants may be available to you – but don't place all your hopes on them, because there may be many catches. Ask about all these potential pitfalls right at the start of the process so that you don't waste time.

Soft loans

Government agencies and charitable trusts can sometimes provide soft loans. These are often based on the same criteria as the grants, but you have to pay the money back. The advantage to you is that you pay little or no interest, making them much cheaper than bank lending. Obviously it's worth trying to get a grant if you can, but in some cases a soft loan will be all that is available to you.

Incubator programmes

Some universities, local authorities and other organizations run 'incubators' for new businesses.

These offer a complete package of support which can include any combination of:

- office/workshop space;
- funding;
- mentor;
- receptionist service;
- telephone line;
- mailing address;
- training;
- computer systems;
- networking events.

It is well worth finding out about such services in your local area. Start with a search on the web, or ask your local business link.

However, all this doesn't always come free (or even cheaply). Many incubators will want to be given shares in your business in return for their services, and you need to weigh up:

1. Whether the number of shares they want represents an expensive way for you to buy the services you are getting – and specifically the services you value.

2. Whether the people who run the incubator are the kind of people you want to be involved in your business permanently until you sell it, or at least long-term, until you can afford to buy them out.

F. BLAGGING

This doesn't tend to be mentioned anywhere else as a source of funding your business, but I think it's one of the most important things for entrepreneurs to do.

First, let's be clear on a definition. When I say 'blagging' I mean:

- Trying to get things cheaply or free.

- Trying to get things in return for favours or offering something else in return that has no cash cost to you.

- Borrowing things.

Entrepreneurs have to keep the costs in their companies as low as possible, so blagging is a vital tool.

Whenever you need something in your business, particularly at the seed, start-up or turnaround phases, think 'How can I blag this?' before you reach for your company credit card to pay for something. This then removes cost out of your business plan, providing you with an indirect source of funding. Blagging is not a one-way street, however. The most successful blaggers get results because people owe them favours. It really pays off to do whatever you can to help other people – even if you can't see a possible benefit to you at the time. Just be nice to people, help them out – and one day, in some way, it will come back to benefit you.

Don't be the kind of person who is always on the take – always be giving, and then people will always want to be offering things to you. That is the best way to be a good blagger.

6

CHAPTER SIX

Sources of funding

In Chapter 5 we discussed the types of funding available to you, and in this chapter we're going to look at all the different places you can go to obtain the funding.

About the star ratings

Each source of finance is rated as follows:

Star ratings	
Ease of application	The more stars you see here, the easier it is to apply for the funding. Fewer stars mean lots of paperwork, lots of difficult questions, lots of hoops to jump through – and generally a lot of hassle!
Chances of success	Five stars here mean that, if you have a good business with a good opportunity, you stand a really good chance of raising the funding from this source. Fewer stars mean that it can be tough. That may mean that the process is difficult, or simply that so many businesses apply for a limited resource.

Risk level to you	A high number of stars here means that the type and source of funding is relatively low risk to you, while fewer stars denote that you could lose your house, savings or other things that are important to you if things go wrong.
Cost	The cost of different types of finance is difficult to compare – for equity investment you won't actually give any of your money to the investor, but years later they will perhaps take away twice as much money as they put in. For debt finance, however, you pay interest and fees from the moment you take the debt on. I'm going to focus on the money you actually have to spend in the day-to-day running of the company on the type and source of finance in question – not the comparison between what the funders put in and what they take out.
Suitability for seed stage	The more stars in each of these rows, the better the source of finance is suited to that stage of business. Five stars is pretty much perfect, one star means best avoided.
Suitability for start-ups	
Suitability for early stage	
Suitability for expanding businesses	
Suitability for turnarounds	

About the examples

Most businesses use a mixture of the sources of funding listed here, so some companies are used as examples under more than one source. I highly recommend mixing and matching your funding in this way too.

CUSTOMERS

We have discussed how customers can help to fund your business by paying money to you in advance or by buying more; and that this is the best possible way of obtaining the funds you need. Small businesses, however, are often surprised to find that their customers are interested in investing in them in other ways. They might want to encourage competition among suppliers if their existing suppliers give them bad service or bad value, perhaps they really value the work you do for them already and are keen to support your growth, or they may be really excited by the new product or service you plan to offer. In this case they may well give you a loan or buy shares in order to help your business get off the ground.

Funding types

The main funding type to focus on here is sales:

1. Ask customers to pay in full or in part in advance for their orders to provide you with substantial cash flow benefits.

2. Ask them to pay a deposit on their orders to improve your cash flow.

3. Try to up-sell extra products or services to them.

4. Negotiate longer-term contracts with them.

If this doesn't work, or isn't enough, you may also be able to try:

- **Debt.** Ask customers to lend you money at a good interest rate in return for priority treatment and high-quality service.

- **Equity.** Offer them the opportunity to buy shares in your company.

- **Blagging.** They might let you use some of their facilities. Some entrepreneurs have worked from a spare desk at their customer's office for the first few months while they get started.

We'll focus on getting funding from your customers through sales.

Who's it suitable for?

All business types and stages.

What do they want?

They have good cash flow, but they want to improve margins and getting a discount from you by paying in advance is attractive to them. They are also likely to be interested in having a new supplier who is prepared to work more closely with them to understand their business and to deliver on promises. It's amazing how many suppliers let their customers down on a regular basis.

How do you get it?

Ask. Many people are shy about doing this because they think the customer will reject the idea – but you'd be surprised how many businesses are funded in this way.

Emphasize the benefits that your business will bring them compared to their existing suppliers. Show them that it is worth backing you because of these benefits. If you are running an existing business and are seeking money for growth, be sure not to suggest that you could be on the verge of going out of business if you don't get the funding from them, because then they may panic and start looking for other suppliers.

What to ask

- Please?

Pros/cons

+ It can be a very cheap source of funding.

+ It's very easy to apply for.

+ It can be arranged relatively quickly.

+ Your customer then has a real interest in seeing you succeed!

+ Having this kind of funding is like a magnet for other investors such as business angels, banks, etc. If your customers are prepared to invest even small amounts in you it is a great sign of the potential of your business. They'll be like moths to a flame.

− Your customer will expect preferential treatment (not too much of a negative this one).

− You'll have to be careful not to give other customers the idea that you are too much in this customer's pocket.

Case study

Cliff Stanford, founder of Demon Internet, shows that this kind of funding can also work for consumer companies:

Around 1991, on an internet bulletin board, a number of people made the comment that we'd never get low cost internet access in the UK. However, I made the comment that if 200 of us got together then it could be done at a cost per head of about £10 per month. A lot of people were keen but I said I'd need about £20,000 to set the company up, and I would need to know I had customers. So, about 150 people sent me cheques for £120, and they didn't know who I was! So there was a market there.

Cliff set up the business, and later sold it for around £30m.

Star ratings	
Ease of application	***** Just ask.
Chances of success	**** Pretty high.
Risk level to you	**** Generally low if you take advance payments and do actually deliver. Can be higher risk if you accept a loan or equity investment.
Cost	***** Perhaps some discount but that's it.
Suitability for seed stage	*** Perfect, but you may not yet know who your customers will be.
Suitability for start-ups	***** Perfect.
Suitability for early stage	***** Perfect.
Suitability for expanding businesses	***** Perfect.
Suitability for turnarounds	***** Perfect.

YOU

Entrepreneurs often invest some of their own money or assets in the business, and this will generally be expected by other investors. However, you need to be careful not to throw everything you have in the world into the company. None of the investors wants you to live in poverty.

A venture capitalist once told me that he liked to see that the entrepreneur would feel a little pain if the business collapsed, but that he didn't want the entrepreneur spending all their waking hours worrying about paying the mortgage or where their children's next meal was coming from – that only serves to divert their attention away from the business.

Your investors won't want you to get yourself into huge debt, or invest every penny of your savings, but they will want to see some evidence that you believe in your business and its opportunity as much as you say you do – and the best indication of this is that you are willing to stake a relatively large sum of money on it. The word 'relatively' is important here, because if you are the eighth earl of Milton Keynes with a huge family fortune and a vast (but perfectly square) estate, then you will be expected to invest more in your company than if you have just left university with a great business idea but a bank balance that looks as if you've been financing a major international war.

So what could you invest?

- Some of your savings.

- Some of your assets.

- Money raised from assets – re-mortgaging your house, selling your car.

- Your time – work for a low salary for the first year or two.

- Personal security – give a personal guarantee on the bank loan (be sure to read the section on security later, see pp. 192–4).

Other investors are only really interested in what you are putting into the business now, alongside their investment. So if you're raising money for an established company you may need to put in something more yourself in order to show your commitment. This is an important reason not to invest everything you have in this funding stage, because if you go back to funders in a year and ask for more money they may expect you to put more in as well, which you may not be able to afford if you have over-invested at this stage. It is vital, however, that you make sure you're raising enough to cover the business for any problems that may arise until you expect to have enough cash flow to fund the company.

Self-funding by the entrepreneur is how sole-traders and partnerships are often financed, as well as lots of start-up and very early-stage limited companies. Even if you don't have lots of money, there is nothing to stop you taking on personal debt in order to invest in your business.

Now this, of course, has to be followed by a serious warning: small businesses are risky. You will know the risk involved in your business better than anybody else, so it is up to you to judge how much of your own money to invest, and how much personal debt to take on to invest in your company. Consider what would happen if your business didn't work. What would happen to your personal finances if the money you put in wasn't repaid? If you'd lose everything it's not worth it – spread the risk around a number of forms of funding instead. It will often be a requirement of other funders that you do have some kind of financial stake in the business, however, so how can you raise this money personally?

Savings and investments

Do you have money in a savings account, or other investments in shares that you could sell?

Re-mortgage your house

If you've been diligently paying off your mortgage for years then, along with the rise in house prices, you should have a good amount of equity available in your property. It can be a good source of finance for your business. Do be aware of the charges you may have to pay to release this money – valuation fees, solicitors' costs, penalties if you move mortgage provider, etc. – but you may be able to negotiate a better interest rate. Finally, be warned (as in the adverts) that you are risking your home by taking out any debts secured against it. Be sure that you can make the repayments even if your business doesn't work out.

Take out an unsecured personal loan

If you have a good credit record then personal finance companies are desperate to throw money at you – and interest rates are currently relatively low. Be aware that even though the loan is unsecured, if you are unable to keep up repayments you will be taken to court.

Use credit cards – the five-card trick

This is highly risky and can be expensive, but quite a few entrepreneurs have got their business off the ground in this way. Use your credit card to pay for things your business needs, and then keep moving the balance between low or zero interest deals on other cards. But be warned, credit cards are an extremely expensive form of finance if you are not on one of the very special deals; and the special deals are much harder to get now than they used to be.

You should use a type of finance that is appropriate to what you want to use the money for. For instance, there's no point re-mortgaging the house if you only need the money in your business for a couple of months, and it's a very bad idea to use your credit card for long-term funding.

How to invest the money

You can put the money into your business by buying shares, or by lending the money to the company. Your accountant will be able to advise you on the best option, depending on your personal circumstances and the future plans for the company.

Star ratings	
Ease of application	***** Just ask.
Chances of success	***** How could you refuse yourself?
Risk level	* Not so good – you could be in a bad situation if things don't work out.
Cost	*** Personal debt can be quite expensive, especially credit cards. And even if you use your savings, this money could have been used to pay off your mortgage early or pay down other debt, therefore saving you a lot of interest.
Suitability for seed stage	*** Perfect, but you may not yet know who your customers will be.
Suitability for early stage	***** Perfect.
Suitability for start-ups	***** Perfect.
Suitability for growth businesses	**** Great, but you may not be able to put much in as a proportion of the overall funding required.
Suitability for turnarounds	***** Perfect. Show some commitment but don't risk everything you have

FAMILY

Those people who have loved you enough to put up with you in the 'dirty nappy' phase, the 'terrible twos' phase and the 'terrible teens' phase, as well as funding you throughout a large part of your life, will believe in you and want to see you succeed.

Funding types

- **Debt.** They could lend you money at a low interest rate (they might offer to lend you money at no interest, in which case accept it, but surprise them with a bonus or a present once it's paid off).

- **Equity.** They could also buy shares in your company.

- **Blagging.** Could they let you use their garage as a workshop, or borrow their car? How else could they help you?

Who's it suitable for?

Entrepreneurs whose families have some spare cash available that would not affect their life if it were lost for ever. This last point is very important, as you do not want to borrow your grandmother's last pennies, only to find your business doesn't work and your grandmother is consequently forced to sell her house to survive. It has to be *spare* money and not their pension, their holiday savings, etc. This means that not all entrepreneurs will have access to this kind of funding. Because this type of funding is generally limited to small amounts, it is mainly suited to start-up businesses.

What do they want?

They want the best for you, which means they may not be looking out for their own needs adequately in this transaction. That means you need to look after them. Make sure there is a written agreement about the arrangement, setting out the interest rate, terms of the loan, repayment plan, etc.

How do you get it?

You could approach just one wealthy family member, or you could spread the risk/opportunity around and, for example, borrow £500 from ten different family members in order to raise £5000.

What to ask

Can you really afford to lose this money if anything goes wrong? Will it affect our good relationship if anything goes wrong?

Pros/cons

✚ It is easy to apply for.

✚ It can be quite easy to succeed in raising funds through this route.

− This type of funding is generally only available in small amounts.

− It is difficult to do business with relations without causing friction.

− Family members who invest may feel they have a right to dictate how you run your business.

Useful contacts

Anyone in your family tree.

Case studies

Jeff Bezos, the founder of amazon.com, funded the company himself for its first six months of operation, but he soon needed more cash. He approached his father, Miguel, who agreed to invest just over $100,000 in February 1995 – enough money to allow Amazon to move out of Jeff's garage and into offices.

Google raised $1m ($1m = £567,300 at the time of writing) in its very first funding round, with the first $100,000 coming from a wealthy entrepreneur. A large proportion of the rest was raised by many family members investing small amounts. At the time of writing, roughly eight years after the company was formed the company is valued at over $120bn, so I think their families will be quite pleased they believed in young Sergey and Larry.

Star ratings	
Ease of application	***** Really easy.
Chances of success	**** Pretty high if your family is well off.
Risk level	** You could fall out with family members if things go wrong.
Cost	***** Very low cost.
Suitability for seed stage	**** Very good.
Suitability for start-ups	**** Very good.
Suitability for early stage	*** Good, but may be a limited amount in comparison to what you need to raise.
Suitability for growth businesses	** Unlikely to be able to raise enough cash.
Suitability for turnarounds	*** Good for turnarounds in the early stages of business, otherwise may not be able to raise enough. Be sure to make clear the current state of the business and the risks involved.

FRIENDS

The people who have seen you through the highs and lows of your life. They've been there at your parties, and they've been there as a shoulder to cry on (hopefully separate occasions!).

Funding types

- **Debt.** They could lend you money at a low interest rate.
- **Equity.** They could buy shares in your business.
- **Blagging.** They may also be able to lend or give you useful things or services either cheaply or free, as a favour.

Who's it suitable for?

Mainly start-up businesses, and of course you'll need some friends with spare cash.

Who provides it?

Your friends – but remember, only the ones who wouldn't fall into difficulties if the money was never repaid. It has to be *spare* cash.

What do they want?

They want to support you in your venture, but they will also probably want some financial return. That means interest on the money or being able to buy shares. However, it could also mean cheap or free products or services from your business as a form of payback – particularly if you're begging or borrowing something from them.

How do you get it?

Remember to ask only the ones who wouldn't fall into difficulties if the money were never repaid. It has to be spare cash. Deal with this professionally and present your business plan to them, giving them the chance to examine and question your plans. Draw up a formal agreement for their investment.

What to ask

Can you really afford to lose this money if anything goes wrong? Will we lose our friendship if anything goes wrong?

Pros/cons

✚ It is easy to apply for.

✚ It can be a cheap source of funding.

− It may affect your friendship if your business doesn't go to plan.

− You may discover that your friends are very different people once money is involved.

Case study

The Subway sandwich bar chain was founded when Fred DeLuca was wondering how to pay his way through college. He went with his parents to visit some family friends and chatted it over with them. They suggested he should open a sandwich bar, and the idea was discussed all night, including the menu and the prices. At the end of the night they were so impressed by Fred's enthusiasm that they handed him a cheque for $1000 to set up the business, and gave him a target of opening 32 stores in ten years.

Star ratings	
Ease of application	***** Really easy.
Chances of success	**** Pretty high.
Risk level	*** You could fall out with valued friends if things go wrong.
Cost	***** Very low cost.
Suitability for seed stage	**** Very good.
Suitability for start-ups	**** Very good.
Suitability for early stage	*** Pretty good, but may not be able to raise enough.
Suitability for expanding businesses	** Unlikely to be able to raise enough cash.
Suitability for turnarounds	*** Good for turnarounds in the early stages of business, otherwise may not be able to raise enough. Be sure to make clear the current state of the business and the risks involved.

CONTACTS/BUSINESS ANGELS

These could be people that you have met at business functions or social occasions, friends of friends, people you deal with at other companies and so on. You have established some sort of basic relationship with them and exchanged contact details, or you know how to contact them through someone else. You are aware that they may have an interest in your line of business. This could also extend beyond your direct line of contacts to the contacts of other people you know. Use your network. Keep your ear to the ground and be aware of who knows whom. This is one of the commonest ways of funding entrepreneurial companies, and it is how I have tended to fund my businesses.

For more information on Business Angels, see the Business Angel Networks section.

Funding types

- **Equity**. If they decide to invest in your company by buying shares, then they are effectively business angels, so treat the process like that for business angel networks, which we will discuss in more detail below.

- **Debt**. They may be prepared to lend you money at a good rate of interest. This will have the advantage to you of being unsecured, whereas the banks will probably require security.

- **Blagging**. What can you blag from your extended network of contacts?

Who's it suitable for?

Mainly companies at start-up, or for those which are still fairly early stage, although it could also be a useful route for growth or turnaround companies.

What do they want?

Their motivations will range from wanting to make money out of their investment in you, to wanting to help the next generation of entrepreneurs, wanting to support another local business, or just wanting to have some fun.

How do you get it?

Get out there and get networking as much as possible, and when there is enough rapport with someone, put the idea to them. Ask your friends and colleagues to introduce you to people who might prove useful.

What to ask

1. What is your main motivation for this investment?

2. How much hands-on involvement do you want?

3. When do you expect to be able to exit?

Pros/cons

+ These people are likely to have business experience and contacts that can help you.

+ Successful people believing in you and your business will carry a lot of weight with other investors (especially your bank), helping you to promote this investment.

− They may be strong characters who would want to have some control in the business.

Useful contacts

Your stash of business cards.

Case studies

Innocent Drinks, the fruit smoothie manufacturer, needed to raise £250,000 to start up. The three founders had no idea how to get the money, so they contacted everyone they knew to ask whether any of them knew anyone rich who might be interested in investing in their business. One friend of theirs got back in touch with a suggestion of a wealthy business person who did invest in small companies. Innocent made their pitch and got their funding.

Jeff Bezos' initial funding for amazon.com came from his own pocket, and an investment by his father, but the company soon needed more money. He approached friends in the investment community (he had previously been an investment banker) and asked them to put him in touch with people they knew who might invest. The process took a lot of work, and Jeff was not a great presenter, but some of the investors could see that he had something special and that there was a real opportunity. By the end of 1995 he had persuaded about 20 individuals to write cheques that added up to $981,000, giving them just under 20 per cent of the company.

Sergey Brin and Larry Page had developed a working prototype of Google, but needed money to buy hardware and recruit more people in order to grow. One of their professors at Stanford University knew of a wealthy local businessman who might be interested in helping them. Andy Bechtolsheim had been one of the founders of Sun Microsystems (another spin out company from the university), and the professor put them in touch with him.

The meeting was on the porch of their professor's house, very early in the morning, and it was brief because Andy had another meeting to go to. But he was immediately impressed with the two founders, and that they had spent the time and their own money to get the prototype together (he thought the business had the right talent and opportunity). Before he dashed off he scribbled out a cheque to Google Inc. for $100,000 and handed it over. Sergey and Larry were thrilled, but had one small problem – they hadn't formed a company yet. So they then had to rush around for a couple of weeks to incorporate the company and open a bank account before they could cash the cheque. Andy later introduced them to many other highly useful contacts to help them expand the business.

Star ratings	
Ease of application	** You'll need to put some work into getting the message around your contacts network, and you may need to meet a lot of people before you land a success, plus you need to get to know the people.
Chances of success	*** If you have a good network already this will be easier.
Risk level	**** You haven't put up any security so can't lose everything – but make sure that it is someone you can work with – particularly in terms of equity investment. For a loan make sure a proper agreement is put in place so that full repayment can't be demanded at short notice.
Cost	**** Pretty low cost.
Suitability for seed stage	**** Very good.
Suitability for start-ups	**** Very good.
Suitability for early stage	**** Very good.
Suitability for expanding businesses	*** Good if you can raise enough, or get lots of people to club together to invest.

Suitability for turnarounds	**** Good for turnarounds, particularly if you can bring in advisers. Be sure to make clear the current state of the business and the risks involved.

SUPPLIERS

In the same way that your customers may be keen to support you in order to improve their supplier base, or access your exciting new product or service, suppliers will also be interested in increasing their customer base.

Enterprising companies can be persuaded to help new customers start up in business by providing them with credit, discounts, a loan or even equity investment. Established businesses can also try for more discount or longer payment terms.

Funding types

- **Blagging**. At its simplest, you simply ask them to support your new venture by extending you more discount or longer payment terms. That means that you end up either saving money or improving your cash flow, both of which will help with the funding of your business.

- **Equity**. You will sometimes find that a supplier may be interested in having more involvement in your new venture. You may open up a new market for them, you may be a great case study for their products which they can use to persuade other potential customers to buy, or you may offer something else that encourages them to invest in you.

- **Debt**. They may be prepared to lend you money to help you start or expand.

Let's focus here on blagging better terms for your purchases from them.

Who's it suitable for?

Seed, start-up, early-stage or growth companies and companies in turn-around.

What do they want?

- A good new customer.

- A new market for their products or services.

- A close working relationship.

- A case study to use to market their services to other customers.

How do you get it?

You have to use all your charm, and build a good relationship with your supplier. Their natural reaction will be not to trust new start-ups, insisting on payment in advance and a low initial discount. But if you can interest them in your plans and give them confidence in you and your abilities then some suppliers can be swayed. It can help if you can get someone who already has a good relationship with them to introduce you.

If you're putting together the funding to turn around an existing business then it can be worth having a word with some of your closer, trusted suppliers. If they can see that you have a good plan, and if they trust you, they will help you to achieve the turnaround. But you have to be very open and show that you are worthy of trust.

What to ask

Will you help me to launch/expand/turnaround my business in return for my loyal custom or help with marketing your products?

Pros/cons

- ✦ Very cheap, or free, source of finance.

- ✦ You will have a very close relationship with a key supplier.

- ✦ A supplier supporting your business is a very good sign to other funders, and even a small contribution from them could help you raise other funding more easily.

– You will be tied to this supplier and feel they have done you a huge favour. It will be difficult to confront them about any problems with their products or services, and difficult to take your business elsewhere.

Useful contacts

Your supplier base.

Case studies

Marks & Spencer were at a key stage of growth when they ran into financial difficulties. One of their main suppliers was a Yorkshire-based textiles company, I. J. Dewhirst, and the management team approached Dewhirst's management to ask for help. Dewhirst readily agreed to extend payment terms (and this was when M&S was a small retailer, so they didn't have the power to pressure suppliers like they have today), to give M&S the cash flow help they needed. As we all know, Marks & Spencer survived and grew into a major retailer – and rewarded Dewhirst with 100 years of absolute loyalty.

Subway sandwich bars also ran into difficulties, after opening only one store. Fred DeLuca, the founder, couldn't afford to pay all his suppliers each week. He adopted a policy of paying as much as he could to each supplier, and taking them the cheque in person. He would meet the business owner, chat to them about the business, give them feedback on the products and hand them the cheque. Then they would place the next week's order then and there. This supplier finance allowed them to open a second store, which gave them increased presence in the local market, and sales increased at the first store as soon as the second store opened. This was the beginning of their success in business.

Star ratings	
Ease of application	**** Simply ask, but it's easier if you already have a contact there.
Chances of success	*** It's easier to get extended credit or discount than the other options – although less enterprising suppliers will be even harder on start-ups or other new customers and you won't get extended payment terms until you've been dealing with them a while.
Risk level	***** Low risk.
Cost	***** Very low cost.
Suitability for seed stage	**** Very good, but you may not need many suppliers yet.
Suitability for start-ups	***** Perfect, but you'll have to use all your charms to persuade them they can trust you.
Suitability for early stage	***** Perfect.
Suitability for expanding businesses	***** Perfect. They'll be keen to keep your business as you grow.
Suitability for turnarounds	**** Ideal, but you'll have to persuade them that your company has a great future.

BUSINESS ANGEL NETWORKS

'Business angel' is the common name for private wealthy individuals who invest in small and medium-sized businesses. Recently the BBC TV series *Dragons' Den* has led to the nickname 'dragons', but I still prefer the term 'angels' as it sounds a lot more friendly and positive – which is generally what these people are like.

On the part of the angels, an investment in small companies is one element of a diversified portfolio of savings and investments offering different risk/reward ratios. They'll have money tied up in pensions, savings accounts, bonds, blue chip equities, investment funds and so on. However, they have enough money in the lower-risk, lower-reward category – they want to diversify their portfolio by investing in some higher-risk, higher-reward opportunities.

They are likely to have some business experience themselves, and want to use this knowledge and experience to identify an opportunity that others have missed, and spot it at an early stage, when it's relatively cheap to get on board. They may have gained this experience through building a business of their own, or they may have been very senior in a large organization that paid them well. The business angels who invested in my business when it was getting off the ground included three entrepreneurs (each with different core skills and contacts), a senior lawyer from a major law firm who had taken very early retirement, an accountant (again, at a very senior level in one of the big five firms) and a director of a large international publishing company.

This highlights another important point: you can assemble a group of angels to invest in your business to put together the funding you need while spreading the risk for them. This also has the advantage of bringing in extra brains that are experienced in different areas. The spread of experience and expertise among the business angels I invited to invest in my business was no coincidence, and I have benefited hugely from their input beyond their simple financial investment.

There are approximately 18,000 active business angels in the UK, investing an estimated £500m each year. They tend to invest amounts between £5k and £100k in companies they get involved in, but you can assemble a syndicate of more than one angel to raise larger amounts.

The National Association of Business Angels has conducted research into the success rates of investments by their members, and found that 20 per cent had an average annual return of over 50 per cent, while 33 per cent made a total loss, with most occupying the middle ground of a small loss, break-even or a smaller return.

Angels are seasoned business-people who aren't scared by the level of risk involved. They are one of the steadiest and most supportive sources of finance available to your business. If you run into trouble the banks will be running the other way, demanding back the money they lent you, but business angels will generally run to help you, rolling up their sleeves to do what needs to be done.

Funding types

- **Equity**. They will buy shares in your company for an agreed amount. The amount of shares is often discussed in percentages. They will be looking to raise the value of those shares by growing the company, and then being able to sell those shares for a large profit. If the company is profitable they are also likely to want to be paid dividends, a way of distributing some of the profits of the company to shareholders in a tax-efficient way. You should have a formal shareholders' agreement.

Who's it suitable for?

This is suitable for start-ups that have a real opportunity, established proven businesses that are looking to expand and troubled businesses that are being turned around. It's not generally suitable for 'lifestyle' businesses – if you plan to open just one shop or one restaurant, for example, this doesn't offer enough growth potential to give a sufficiently high reward for the risk involved.

If you're looking for amounts of over £2m you may want to consider venture capital instead.

What do they want?

Every business angel is different, and has different aims for their investments. That could include any combination of the following:

- An investment that has a chance to make a big return on investment.

- A company that fits their interests or experience.

- A company they feel they can contribute to, adding value through advice and contacts as well as money.

- A company registered, or that will register, under the Enterprise Investment Scheme (EIS) (see Chapter 8 for details) so they can maximize their return and minimize their risk through tax breaks.

- An element of fun, excitement and challenge.

- A company based locally.

- Something to do! Sometimes they have retired or been made redundant with a large payoff and they are looking to create an investment and a job for themselves. This isn't always a good thing, as they may tread on your toes or try to take over in their enthusiasm. Make sure the boundaries are clear.

How do you get it?

Business angels are often members of angel networks or clubs. Your local Business Link will be able to tell you about the clubs in your area, or try searching the web. They hold regular meetings and invite entrepreneurs to come along and pitch their ideas. Contact the administrator of your local group and ask for the chance to present. They are likely to want a meeting with you first.

Different groups have different ways of funding themselves. Some charge the angels to be members, while some charge the entrepreneurs to present. Some charge a fee based on a percentage of any deal that is done, others want to take shares in your business (be wary of this) and some are free because they are organized or supported by government agencies. Make sure you find out about any small print, and are happy with it, before you commit to anything. Once everything is agreed it is likely that a one-page summary of your business proposal will be circulated to the angels to attract them to the meeting, then you will give a brief presentation at the meeting.

Any angels who are interested will then come and talk to you and request a copy of your full business plan and a further meeting for you to give your full presentation.

Once the angel has seen your plan and your presentation, they will be likely to conduct some research of their own. If they decide to invest after this, they will negotiate with you on the amount to be invested and what they will get in return. We will look at this negotiation in more detail in Chapter 8.

Once they commit they will write you a cheque, or transfer the money into your account, and you will issue them with shares in your company in return.

What to ask

- What can you bring to the business apart from the money – in terms of contacts, knowledge, etc.?

- Have you invested in other small businesses before? Can I talk to them?

- What do you want to get out of this investment?

- How long a period are you prepared to invest for before seeking an exit?

- How important are dividends to you, or do you prefer to reinvest in the business?

- How hands-on do you want to be?

Pros/cons

+ They can bring knowledge, experience and contacts.

✚ If they have a good track record it will impress other funders.

✚ Most angels really understand how businesses work and will help you navigate through the more difficult times without panic.

✚ Angels can often be great mentors.

– Some angels are simply looking for a new toy to play with and will keep meddling in your business.

– A few angels have sizeable egos and forceful personalities. Their success may have made them brash and uncompromising. This can cause friction with you and the rest of your team.

Useful contacts

www.venturesite.co.uk
www.angelinvestmentnetwork.co.uk
www.advantagebusinessangels.co.uk
www.bestmatch.co.uk
www.eban.org
www.nationalbusangels.co.uk
www.beerandpartners.com

	Star ratings
Ease of application	*** Fairly straightforward if done through an angel network. A bit more work is required if you approach angels direct.
Chances of success	**** A good business with great management and a good opportunity is quite likely to get funding. There are plenty of angels with plenty of money, but not many great businesses.
Risk level	**** Because this is an equity investment the risk is quite low for you in relation to the money. But angels will be more hands-

	on than any other type of funder, so there could be a risk of personality clashes or differences of opinion.
Cost	*** Different business angel networks have different charges. Some charge a flat fee to put your proposal in front of members (which can be a few thousand pounds), others take a percentage of the money you raise, and some take a mixture of both. You may also need to have an accountant and lawyer to help you through the process.
Suitability for seed stage	**** Very good, but you may still be a bit too small. Will be suitable if your idea clearly has huge growth potential, or you have an excellent track record.
Suitability for start-ups	***** Perfect, one of my favourite forms of finance for start-ups. Brings in brains as well as cash.
Suitability for early stage	***** Perfect.
Suitability for expanding businesses	**** Great. They'll really be able to help you grow your business, as well as providing the money. You may have to assemble a syndicate of angels in order to provide the size of funding you need. The size of funding you need may be too large, however, and you may have to consider venture capital.
Suitability for turnarounds	**** Can be great. An angel experienced in your industry will know what mistakes you are making and be able to help you change your ways and build a solid business.

INVESTMENT EXCHANGES

This is a relatively new idea that seems to be slowly taking off. There are a number of such exchanges (or 'bourses') – including AngelBourse, Sharemark, FundEx and DCXworld.

Funding types

- **Equity.** Investment exchanges are like a cross between the stock market and business angels. Shares in very small, unquoted companies can be traded by approved high net worth individuals. They are much smaller than the established stock markets such as the main market and Alternative Investment Market (AIM) of the London Stock Exchange, and OFEX. They have memberships, or database lists, of potential investors to which they market new investment opportunities. The company lists on the market to raise the funds, and investors can subsequently trade in the shares, so your investor base may change over time, and investors have more reassurance of being able to achieve an exit than they do with simple business angel investments, because there is a simple mechanism for pricing and selling the shares.

Who's it suitable for?

Fast-growth companies that will offer the kind of returns on investment that members of these exchanges will be seeking.

Who provides it?

- **AngelBourse.** They claim to have 1500 investors registered with them directly and access to a further 75,000 qualified investors through a partnership with another financial services provider – and they say this includes 20 per cent of all UK millionaires! They typically arrange finance of between £200k and £2m.

- **Sharemark/ShareStream.** This is a fundraising and sharetrading service from stockbroker The Share Centre. ShareMark is their exchange, listing shares in companies that their committee has allowed on to the market for trading. ShareStream promotes investment opportunities (which may or may not be listed on ShareMark) to a database of potential investors.

- **FundEx.** Operated by Cavendish Management Resources, this seems to be a fairly basic service, but has the advantage of only charging a success fee based on a percentage of funds raised, where other exchanges have fairly chunky fees upfront whether you raise the funds or not. They don't disclose how many members they have.

- **DCXworld.** At the time of writing they have 1000 investors registered with them, but they also market opportuinities through the 'Risk and Reward' newsletter, which is sent to 20,000 of the UK's wealthiest and most successful entrepreneurs and company directors. They claim to be able to raise funding of between £20k and £5m.

What do they want?

Their members want a fairly high return on investment and an opportunity to exit to realize any gains. This exit can be provided through the exchange itself by the investor simply offering the shares for sale on the exchange again, but they may well be looking for a larger-scale exit such as a trade sale or listing on OFEX or AIM.

The exchange will normally conduct thorough checks on your business, either themselves or through the approved intermediary (AI).

How do you get it?

You find an approved intermediary (AI), such as an accountant, lawyer or corporate finance specialist. Lists of the AIs are available on the websites of the exchanges (see 'Useful contacts', below). The AI will help you prepare your company for the process, and prepare the necessary business plan and documentation. This will then be submitted to the exchange for approval. Once approval has been given, the exchange will begin marketing your investment opportunity to its investor database via email, mailings and sometimes even by telephone if there is a very good fit with a particular investor's requirements.

There may be the opportunity to hold an investor meeting at which people can hear more about your plans and ask you questions, if they are interested.

As investors move to the stage of actively considering an investment they will be put in contact with your AI, who will handle the process of registering their interest in, or commitment to, buying shares (this is called book building).

Finally, it will be time for investors to hand over the cash and be issued with shares, and your AI will handle this too, including complying with the legal requirements to check the source of the capital to prevent money laundering.

In the case of Fundex you don't need an AI, as you are able to list your investment opportunity yourself using a simple form on their website.

What to ask

- What is this fundraising process going to cost if we are successful?
- What is it going to cost if we don't succeed?
- How many active investors are there on your market at the moment?

Pros/cons

+ It can be a good training ground for companies that may later be headed for OFEX or AIM.

+ It's a relatively straightforward way of raising larger sums of money.

+ It gives you a more diversified investor base, avoiding concentrating large numbers of shares (and therefore more control) in a few hands.

✚ It can be quite time-efficient for the management team compared to putting together a syndicate of business angels, or preparing for an OFEX or AIM listing.

– It's more expensive than if you were to put a syndicate of business angels together yourself, as you have to pay fees to your AIs and fees to the exchange.

– There may not be enough investors actively trading in the market to create the liquidity in your stock – i.e. it can be hard for investors to sell shares as there aren't enough buyers. This can mean that your share price is stagnant, or that it drops.

– You can't control who can buy shares in your company.

Useful contacts

www.angelbourse.com or 020 7382 4382
www.sharemark.co.uk
www.dcxworld.com
FundEx: www.cmrworld.com/bexchange

Star ratings	
Ease of application	*** Reasonably involved and complicated.
Chances of success	**** A good business with great management and a good opportunity is quite likely to get funding.
Risk level	**** Because this is an equity investment the risk is quite low for you in relation to the money. But there is always a different kind of risk when ownership of a business is shared.
Cost	*** A little bit more expensive than a business angel network, but not too bad.

▶

Suitability for seed stage	** You're probably too small and unproven.
Suitability for start-ups	*** Can be good if you have an excellent team and a great opportunity.
Suitability for early stage	**** Ideal.
Suitability for expanding businesses	***** Excellent.
Suitability for turnarounds	*** Can be great, but you'll need to be able to convince people who don't know you that well – and who may not even meet you – that the company has a great future.

OFEX

OFEX is a trading market in shares for small and medium-sized enterprises, which currently has 156 companies listed. It is used by more experienced, specialist investors looking to balance their portfolio with some higher-risk, higher-return investments.

Funding types

- **Equity.** Investors in the market will buy shares in your company through their stockbrokers. You will never meet many of them! These people are experienced investors, however, so it's not like when your granny bought shares in British Gas when the government privatized the company by floating it on the main stock market.

How does it work?

You work with an approved adviser – an accountant or corporate finance company – to asses your business and prepare your documentation.

You can choose simply to apply for a listing, which means that you aren't immediately raising any funds in the market, or you can have an initial public offering (IPO), which both lists you on the exchange and offers new shares for sale.

Your advisers will then work with an approved stockbroker to place these shares with institutional investors, such as insurance companies and pension trustees, who invest on OFEX. Other shares may be offered to individual investors, your staff, your customers and so on.

Be aware that once you are listed on a stock market such as OFEX there is an ongoing requirement to disclose key information to the market in the proper way, as well as to comply with the regulations of the market and the Financial Services and Markets Act 2000. You will need to have a specialist adviser working with you on an ongoing basis, and it will also require management time. It is a major commitment.

Who's it suitable for?

Businesses with an established track record and the potential for high growth.

What do they want?

- Like any other funders they want to see a great management team with a good opportunity.

- They want to see the potential for rapid growth in the business.

- They want a consistent performance with no unpredicted nasty surprises.

How do you get it?

There are two ways of fundraising on OFEX:

1. A private placement limits you to a maximum of 100 investors but is much cheaper as you don't require a full prospectus, just a straightforward document called a private placement memorandum.

2. An initial public offering allows you to raise funds from a much wider base of investors, and therefore you are likely to raise more money. This process requires you and your advisers to prepare a full prospectus which will take a lot of time and money.

You need to work through an approved intermediary (an 'OFEX corporate adviser') who will be experienced at the process.

They will run a thorough due diligence process on your business and prepare a prospectus for distribution to potential investors. This is a very important legal document, and the wording and numbers will be very carefully checked and rechecked by your advisers.

This document will then be distributed to potential investors to invite them to buy shares. At this point your adviser may take you on a roadshow of large investors, so you can make a presentation and answer questions. You need to prepare for this very carefully.

Your OFEX corporate adviser will usually charge you an initial fee when you appoint them, and then a fee on completion of the fundraising process. OFEX states that the fees are likely to amount to between 5 per cent and 10 per cent of the funds raised. You will then have to pay an annual retainer fee for their continuing advice.

These fees are open to negotitaion, so when appointing advisers you should hold a 'beauty parade' to meet a selection of different firms, to see what they offer, check that you can work with them and negotiate fees.

As well as your OFEX adviser, you will need to retain a lawyer, an accountant, a registrar and a financial PR firm.

The lawyer will help you agree and check the terms of engagement of your team of professional advisers, ensure the company has the proper legal structures and paperwork in place, and will help prepare and check the memorandum of placement or the prospectus. They will also work on behalf of the OFEX adviser, conducting key parts of the due diligence.

The accountant will prepare the necessary financial reports for the prospectus and ensure that the company meets the requirements to list on the market. The accountant will also work for your OFEX adviser to conduct due diligence.

The registrar helps prepare the section of the prospectus relating to the application for shares. They will also deal with any applications for shares, issuing certificates and banking the money for you, plus maintaining the register of shareholders.

The financial PR company will help bring you to the attention of potential investors. They will also help you to meet the requirements of the market with regard to communicating key information about your company during the fundraising process, and on an ongoing basis once you are listed.

What to ask

- How much will this process cost?
- Are you confident you can raise the amount we require?

- Are we ready for this?

- How long will the process take?

- How much management time will be involved?

Pros/cons

+ Easier access to future funding through share placings.

+ The ability to use your shares (instead of cash) to make acquisitions.

− You and your management team will have an awful lot of work to do to prepare for IPO.

− You and your management team will have a lot of work to do to meet the reporting and other requirements that go with a public listing.

Useful contacts

www.ofex.com

Case study

Companies listed on OFEX include Arsenal Holdings plc and Manchester City plc (you may have heard of the football clubs they own?), as well as the Shepherd Neame and Adnams breweries, plus many companies that aren't well known because they operate in very specialist areas.

Star ratings	
Ease of application	** Difficult. There is an awful lot of paperwork to be done, and there are numerous hoops to jump through.
Chances of success	*** If your advisers think you meet the criteria then you are reasonably likely to be able to raise the money you need.
Risk level	*** Not too risky in itself, but the company will then be in the public eye and it is much more difficult to deal with problems in your business without their becoming disasters.
Cost	** Quite costly. Your advisers will not be cheap, and then there are fees to OFEX itself.
Suitability for seed stage	* Not suitable at all.
Suitability for start-ups	** Only suitable in a very few cases.
Suitability for early stage	*** Can be great if you have a good management team and opportunity – but be ready for the extra reporting burden.
Suitability for expanding businesses	**** Can be the ideal route for expanding businesses.
Suitability for turnarounds	* Can be tricky and is best avoided. It's a costly process, and you'll need to have an exceptionally good case for being able to turn the business around. It's best to do turnarounds out of the glare of the markets.

AIM

AIM is the next market up from OFEX, but it is still a level below the full market of the London Stock Exchange. Again, investors are mainly institutions or experienced wealthy individuals. It stands for the 'Alternative Investment Market'.

Funding types

- **Equity.** Investors buy your shares through their brokers.

How does it work?

Just the same as OFEX, but AIM is a bigger and more demanding market for companies.

Who's it suitable for?

Businesses that have really proved themselves. Often companies will start on OFEX, or have been VC (venture capital) funded, before moving up to AIM.

What do they want?

A good return on their money, with a moderate amount of risk.

How do you get it?

Follow the same procedure as for OFEX (see previous section).

In this case your main adviser (which is called your OFEX adviser on OFEX) is called your nominated adviser, known as a 'Nomad', and they will be a corporate finance specialist, an accountant or a broker. Again, you can go down the route of a placing or a public offering.

Listing your company on AIM is a long and complex process, involving even more time, work and money than listing on OFEX. You are likely to incur fees in excess of £250,000, so you need to be raising a substantial amount of money to make it worthwhile. You need to start the process about 18–24 months before you plan to raise the money and list your company.

You will also need to adopt a much higher standard of corporate governance than is required of you as a private company, or even as an OFEX-listed company. This may lead to the founding shareholder feeling that they are losing control of the business, and that it is being run by 'the suits'. You need to be certain that your company, and your management team are at the right stage for a flotation.

What to ask

- How much time and effort will this take for the management team?

- Do you think the company is at the right stage for this yet?

- What kind of valuation will we be able to get for the company?

Pros/cons

+ Increased profile for your company's good news.

+ More liquidity (ease of buying and selling because of number of active traders) than on OFEX.

+ The status of being listed on AIM will mark you out as a major player in your industry.

+ You can use your shares to fund acquisitions.

- Increased profile for your company's bad news.

- Expensive.

- It will take a lot of management time away from the running of the business.

Useful contacts

www.londonstockexchange.com/aim

Case study

Entrepreneurs John Barnes and Richard Richardson have twice floated companies on AIM. The first was Harry Ramsden's Fish and Chips in the early 1990s, when the business was at a very early stage. They had raised the funding to buy the business, which consisted of just one fish and chip restaurant near Leeds in the UK, from an American bank, but the bank wanted to pull out after only a few months because of a change in its investment strategy. John and Richard had to find new funding quickly, and someone suggested they should float the company. They were surpised at first, but took the advice and held an initial public offering to achieve a listing on the Junior Market (now called AIM). The offer was well oversubscribed, because of the huge support in the local area, and they raised all the money they needed to begin rolling Harry Ramsden's restaurants out across the UK. When they sold Harry Ramsden's in 1991, they reinvested the money they made in a new venture – La Tasca Spanish Tapas bars – which they also floated on to AIM because of the positive experience they had the first time around.

Star ratings	
Ease of application	* Very hard work.
Chances of success	*** Pretty good if your advisers are good and believe in your business.
Risk level	*** Raising the funding isn't so risky, but your business will then be scrutinized by the financial press and the investors very carefully, so the stakes are much higher.
Cost	* Expensive.
Suitability for seed stage	* Not suitable at all.
Suitability for start-ups	* Very unlikely to be suitable unless you have an amazing brand, patent or opportunity, plus an amazing management team with a great track record in the sector.
Suitability for early stage	** It's possible, but you have to show that you are a solid company with fantastic prospects for growth.
Suitability for expanding businesses	**** Can be the ideal route for expanding businesses – but you'll need to have a very solid business with an excellent financial team.
Suitability for turnarounds	* Not suitable.

VENTURE CAPITAL FIRMS

Venture capitalists (VC, otherwise known as private equity firms) manage funds of money on behalf of investors who want to be able to invest in entrepreneurial unquoted businesses. These investors may be pension funds, insurance companies or very wealthy individuals. They lack the time and the expertise to work on making lots of relatively small investments in small companies, and they also want to spread their risk by investing in a fund that will in turn invest in a range of different companies, with a range of different risk profiles. They make a return on their investment based on the fortunes of the fund as a whole rather than the fortunes of one company.

Funding types

- **Equity.** A venture capital firm will invest in your business by buying shares. After a period of three to five years they will sell their shares, making a substantial return on their investment. They may also earn dividends on the shares in the interim.

- **Debt.** VCs sometimes provide debt finance, but only ever alongside an equity investment, and normally through special forms of loan that allow them to convert it into equity if they wish.

We'll focus here on raising equity through VCs.

Who's it suitable for?

Companies entering a stage of rapid growth for which a major investment (over £100,000 at the very least, but most firms won't look at anything under £1m) is required, but for which very high returns are possible.

Who provides it?

There are over 170 venture capital firms in the UK, investing several billion pounds each year between them.

What do they want?

- A high annual return on their investment – a rule of thumb is an annual return (known as annual internal rate of return, or IRR) of 20 per cent at minimum, increasing up to 50 per cent on riskier early-stage deals or for more demanding VCs. This rate of return could also come from dividends or tax breaks, and doesn't all have to be generated by an increase in the value of the equity.

- A sensible valuation of the business at its current stage, giving them good value on their investment now, and making it easier to generate a higher rate of return.

- A clear and focused plan that takes into account the most likely risks.

- A clear plan for an exit, probably for within three to five years.

- A solid management team they can believe in – many firms will persuade and help you to recruit if they don't feel you have this yet but they like everything else about your business.

- A seat on the board for a director they nominate, who is likely to be an outsider they hire especially for your project. This person will bring a huge amount of experience and a range of useful contacts.

- A solid commitment to the project from the management team and key staff.

How do you get it?

With the help of your advisers and the BVCA directory (see 'Useful contacts' below) put together a shortlist of VCs to target. In compiling this list, consider the requirements and preferences of each firm and how these fit with your investment opportunity.

Some firms only invest in companies in particular industries, particular geographical areas or at particular stages of a company's growth. The amount of funding you are seeking will also affect which firms you choose.

It's most likely that the firm will want to hear from you directly, rather than your advisers (despite what your advisers say) – as one VC said:

If the entrepreneur can't work out how to get a meeting with me, how are they going to create a multi-million pound fast-growth company?

Some firms prefer to receive just the executive summary at first, and then request the full business plans if they are interested. Either check the information you have on the firm or ask your advisers to help with this.

The next stage is a meeting to discuss your business plan. It is at this meeting that the VCs will be studying the management team carefully, so make absolutely sure that you know the plan inside out and have prepared for all the tough questions. This is a one-chance meeting, so don't blow it.

They may have already conducted some basic investigations into you and your industry, and come up with what they believe is a fair estimate of the valuation of your business.

Now it is time to agree headline terms. The key ones will be the valuation, the amount of funding to be provided, the structure of that funding in terms of equity, debt and asset finance, the timing of that investment, any changes or additions to the management team and any special conditions such as founders to sign new, tougher employment contracts or a patent to be obtained, etc.

Once these headline terms have been agreed by signing an 'offer letter' or 'term sheet' (which is not legally binding on either side, but is a strong indication of commitment), the process of due diligence will begin. This can take some time, particularly if potential problems are found.

If due diligence doesn't throw up any deal-breaking problems it will then be time to negotiate the final terms. The VC is likely to try negotiating down the valuation based on things they have found in due diligence, and you will need to rely on your advisers to fight your corner.

On completion of the negotiations the final documentation will be drawn up. This will normally include a shareholders' agreement, a revised memorandum and articles of association for your company, a disclosure letter in which you formally set out all the important information, and a warranties and indemnities agreement. This last document is likely to involve quite a bit of negotiation between the lawyers on each side, as it has very serious implications should anything go wrong.

On completion of all of this, the VC will invest the money into your company and you will issue the shares and formally appoint their representative to the board.

What to ask

- What can you bring to this company on top of the financial investment? Do you have useful contacts or industry experience?
- Can I talk to the directors of other companies you have funded?

Pros/cons

- ✚ They will give your business credibility and stability.
- ✚ They will bring expertise and contacts as well as money.
- ✚ They will be much more interested in sticking with you through hard times than debt financiers such as banks.
- ✚ Much more interested in growing the business than debt financiers, who simply want it to be able to repay their loan.
- − They will have a lot of money, and their reputation, invested in your business, and if they don't think you're doing your job properly, they'll seek to sideline you or push you out.
- − The day you bring in venture capitalists is the day you agree to sell your business within five years. Is this what you want?

Useful contacts

www.bvca.co.uk is the website of the British Venture Capital Association, and provides a searchable directory of firms. You can also search on the web – but the best way is to ask other entrepreneurs for contacts and introductions.

Star ratings	
Ease of application	* Difficult and time-consuming.
Chances of success	** It's tough, but if you have a good team and a good opportunity you'll be welcomed with open arms.
Risk level	*** Generally low risk, because the VC is as committed to the long-term success of the business as you are, unlike a debt financier who can just call in their loan. However, be careful about what warranties and indemnities you sign!
Cost	** This can be expensive, because the firm will want to charge large fees to your company for its services as well as taking shares, but VCs will go where the banks fear to tread, and your business won't be burdened with debt repayments at a critical time of growth.
Suitability for seed	* Very unlikely to be suitable unless you have an absolutely amazing team with a revolutionary idea – probably in a hot sector such as technology or science.
Suitability for start-ups	* As with seed stage.
Suitability for early stage	*** A good source of funding to help a business develop in its early stages.
Suitability for expanding businesses	**** Can be one of the best sources of funds for fast-growing businesses.

Suitability for turnarounds	**** Can be ideal for this type of business. VCs understand that businesses hit problems, and if you have a clear plan to turn the business around they'll be interested – if the business has the potential to be big enough.

REGIONAL VENTURE CAPITAL FUNDS

The Regional Venture Capital Funds (RVCFs) were set up by Chancellor Gordon Brown to provide funding to small and medium-sized businesses seeking amounts below £500,000. Previously it had been difficult to secure this kind of amount, because it was too large for a standard bank loan or business angel investment – but also too small for normal venture capitalists to consider.

The main regions in England (North-East, North-West, Yorkshire and the Humber, East Midlands, West Midlands, East of England, London, South-East and South-West) each have their own locally managed fund, which is overseen centrally by the Small Business Service.

Funding types

- **Equity.** Very much like a normal venture capital fund, except they can deal in smaller amounts, and they are focused on your local area.

Who's it suitable for?

Some start-ups with good growth potential, early-stage businesses and growth businesses.

Who provides it?

Your local RVCF can be contacted through your Business Link. It gets its funds from private investment funds and the government.

What do they want?

Much the same as normal venture capitalists but on a slightly smaller scale to go with the smaller amounts of funding. Due diligence is likely to be a bit less harsh, for instance. But the RVCFs will be run by professional venture capitalists, so they won't just be a soft touch. As they are brand new at the time of writing, it remains to be seen exactly what their investment criteria and process will be.

How do you get it?

Through your business advisers or your local Business Link. Once in contact with the RVCF, the process will be similar to a normal venture capitalist, and it won't do you any harm to show that you are taking the process just as seriously.

What to ask

The same as for venture capital firms.

Pros/cons

The same as for venture capital firms.

	Star ratings
Ease of application	** More straightforward than a standard VC, but still likely to take a lot of work.
Chances of success	*** Reasonably good if you have a good team and a good opportunity, with prospects for growth.
Risk level	**** Relatively low, but again watch out for what you are signing your name to!
Cost	** We've yet to see how demanding the RVCFs will be in terms of the valuation and size of stake they get for their investment, but it's still likely to be relatively expensive.

▶

Suitability for seed	* Unlikely to be suitable unless there's something special about you.
Suitability for start-ups	** Will be good if you have really good growth prospects.
Suitability for early stage	**** Excellent.
Suitability for expanding businesses	*** If you don't need tonnes of cash it could be a very good option.
Suitability for turnarounds	**** Great potential.

THE BIG BANKS

And now, everybody's favourite funding source – the major high street banks. But am I being sarcastic? Sadly not. This really is the first, and only, place that most entrepreneurs go to raise finance – and as a result they don't need to offer you very competitive deals in order to win your business.

When it comes to starting or expanding a business most people just arrange a meeting with their existing bank manager and go along and ask nicely – 'Please will you sell me a loan at higher than necessary interest rates? OK, that's not what they actually say, but they might as well.

How do I know this? Because that's what I've done in the past before I knew better, and that's what lots of my friends have done – and our experiences are backed up by endless surveys. It takes a good few years of experience as an entrepreneur before you realize that there are other ways to raise money.

So don't have the limiting belief that the banks are the place to get money, and that they are doing you an amazing favour if they lend it to you. Just consider them as one of the many options and weigh them up with the competition on price and service.

It's also worth understanding that you aren't restricted to raising funds from the bank where you hold your current account. You can shop around any of the high street banks, who will all be pleased to sell to you if you are considered a good risk.

Equally, don't have the limiting belief that the bank is just looking for a reason to justify saying 'no' to you. Banks only make money if they say 'yes' to lending you money (and you pay them back). Therefore, their managers are rewarded on meeting targets for selling a certain number of loans or overdrafts. It is in their interests to say 'yes' to you – so if they say 'no', there will be reason. It could be that the risk is too high, they don't have confidence in you, they don't believe the market for your services is solid enough – or it could just be that they don't understand.

If they say 'no', make sure you get as much feedback as you can, and use it to prepare your new pitch to a different bank manager. The big advantage is that there are a lot of them out there, so you can just keep trying.

Funding types

The high street banks can offer you debt finance and often asset finance too. They make their money by selling these products, and earn money by charging interest, and charging fees for setting up the facility, renewing it, arranging security or breathing (joke). The fees do add up, but often they are a relatively small percentage of the sum they lend you. This low reward means that they really only consider relatively low-risk ventures. The challenge comes because your bank manager's idea of low risk can be very different from yours.

As well as their standard loans and overdrafts, some of the high street banks offer the government's Small Firms Loan Guarantee Scheme (SFLGS). More of this on p. 193.

Who's it suitable for?

Start-ups and early-stage companies can get some funding from the bank, but growth companies are likely to be able to negotiate better rates. Turnaround companies will find it hard unless you have some assets such as property or machinery that they can take as security against the debt.

Who provides it?

HSBC, Barclays, Lloyds TSB, RBS/Natwest, Bank of Scotland/Halifax.

What do they want?

- Low risk.

- Profitable business (for them).

- The opportunity to sell you more stuff (they'll try to get you to take out life insurance with them and all sorts of other things while you are trying to arrange a loan).

- As much security as possible. They'll ask for personal guarantees, etc. Resist. (See Chapter 8, 'Negotiating the deal'.)

How do you get it?

Arrange a meeting at your local branch, present your business plan, answer questions, fill out some forms.

In many cases now, the manager won't be allowed to make the decision on your application; they simply write up a report and send it to a central unit, where people that you will never meet make the decision. This seems strange when one of the most important parts of the decision is your personality, attitude and talent – the bit they don't get to see.

In other cases the manager might be authorized to make lending decisions on amounts of up to, say, £30,000. But if you apply for a loan of £31,000 they have to refer it to a more senior colleague. It might be better to arrange to meet that colleague.

If the only stumbling block is that you can't offer them enough security, direct them towards the SFLGS.

What to ask

- Are you the manager I will always be able to deal with on this issue?

- Do you have the final decision on this application, or do you just write a report and send it to a central unit for the decision to be made there?

- Do you have enough lending authority to make this decision?

Pros/cons

✚ Easy to access, just nip to your local branch.

✚ Reasonably easy to obtain the finance.

✚ Debt finance is relatively cheap.

- Debt finance from high street banks is more expensive than elsewhere.

- They will demand lots of security.

- They will only be a fair weather friend. If you hit problems, the bank is most likely to add to those rushing to get their money out.

- You may get frustrated at not being able to deal with the actual people who make the decisions.

Useful contacts

www.hsbc.co.uk
www.barclays.co.uk
www.rbs.co.uk
www.natwest.co.uk
www.lloydstsb.co.uk
www.hbos.co.uk

	Star ratings
Ease of application	**** Fairly easy, just a meeting and a few forms. The frustrating bit is that many of the banks make you meet a 'relationship' manager, who then sends the details to the person who actually makes the decision – and you're not allowed to even speak to them on the phone.
Chances of success	**** Pretty high.
Risk level	** If things go wrong you could end up losing any security you have given and getting a bad credit rating.
Cost	** You can generally get everything cheaper somewhere else.

Suitability for seed	* Try to avoid getting into debt at this stage, but bank funding might be suitable if you really need it.
Suitability for start-ups	*** Quite suitable, but there are cheaper sources outside of the high street.
Suitability for early stage	**** Suitable as part of the funding mix, but do shop around and consider smaller banks.
Suitability for expanding businesses	*** Debt is a useful part of the funding mix for expanding businesses, but there are cheaper and more flexible sources. An expanding business is best working through a corporate finance specialist to arrange debt.
Suitability for turnarounds	** The banks are wary of risk, and your cash flow and balance sheet may not be great. Also, you don't want to saddle the business with debt if you can avoid it.

ALTERNATIVE DEBT PROVIDERS

If you want to raise debt finance, make sure you shop around, and this includes the banks you don't normally think of – the smaller ones, or the ones that used to be building societies. You can often get a much better deal, with a more personal service.

Funding types

Exactly the same as high street banks, but generally cheaper and more straightforward. They can normally provide you with loans, overdrafts, a commercial mortgage and some forms of asset finance. For SFLGS you will probably need to go through one of the main banks, however.

Who's it suitable for?

Start-up and early-stage businesses mostly.

Who provides it?

The Co-operative Bank
Alliance & Leicester
The Bank of Ireland (not just in Ireland)
Northern Bank (in Northern Ireland)
European Venture Partners

Keep an eye out for others!

What do they want?

Very much the same as the main banks, but they are more competitive.

How do you get it?

The same as with the high street banks.

What to ask

- How are you different from the main high street banks?

- Plus the same questions you would ask the main banks.

Pros/cons

+ Because fewer business owners think to go to these banks, they are more competitive in order to attract custom.

+ Some have an ethical policy.

+ They are generally cheaper.

+ They can be easier to deal with because they are smaller and more straightforward.

− They may not have the infrastructure you need for international payments, BACS payments, internet banking, etc.

− With many smaller banks it can take a couple of days longer for payments into your account to clear because the main banks won't let the smaller banks into the clearing system. Thus they have to bank with one of the major banks themselves and clear payments through them.

Useful contacts

www.alliance-leicestercommercialbank.co.uk
www.co-operativebank.co.uk/business
www.bankofireland.co.uk/business_banking/
www.nbonline.co.uk – the Northern Bank
www.evp.co.uk

And I know that First Direct is considering launching a business banking product, so do check **www.firstdirect.co.uk** too.

You can also find alternative providers through your accountant or a corporate finance specialist.

Star ratings	
Ease of application	**** Generally straightforward.
Chances of success	**** Pretty high.
Risk level	** If things go wrong you could end up losing any security you have given, and having a bad credit rating.
Cost	***** Low cost.
Suitability for seed	** Try to avoid getting into debt at this stage, but these banks may be the best source if you really need to.
Suitability for start-ups	***** Very suitable.
Suitability for early stage	**** Very suitable, but check they can meet your needs in terms of internet banking, types of payment, etc.
Suitability for expanding businesses	* Unlikely to be suitable for businesses with a large turnover and diverse banking needs.
Suitability for turnaround	* Unlikely to have the expertise to support you.

ASSET FINANCE COMPANIES

These are companies that specialize in this field of finance and are independent of the banks who also often have an asset finance division.

How does it work?

Instead of you going out to buy a fancy new piece of machinery, or a computer network, or a couple of company vehicles, the asset finance company buys them for you.

You then pay a monthly fee for the use of the asset, and depending on the form of finance it may become yours at the end of the agreed period.

The different forms of asset finance are leasing, hire purchase or hire. See Chapter 5 for more information on each.

Some firms also offer commercial mortgages.

Who's it suitable for?

This can be an excellent way to help fund a growing business. Although it is also very suitable for start-ups, it can be difficult for very early-stage companies to get asset finance, but it's worth a go.

Who provides it?

Specialist asset finance companies that you can approach directly, but in some cases the vendor of the asset you are buying will have a deal with an asset finance company. Do be sure to shop around for the best deal.

What do they want?

- A creditworthy business that they believe will continue to make the repayments.
- To fund an asset that they can take away if you don't continue to

make the repayments, and that will still have a value when sold secondhand.

How do you get it?

Your accountant or Business Link adviser can put you in touch with asset finance companies, either in your area or in your industry sector. Alternatively, ask the vendor of the item if they have a relationship with an asset finance provider.

It will be hard for a new company to raise finance through leasing. An established company will need to provide a set of full-year accounts, and the finance provider will be looking to see that your balance sheet is strong enough, i.e. that you don't have too much debt already.

What to ask

- Which form of asset finance do you think is most suitable for my needs?

- What happens if I want to buy/keep the asset at the end of the term?

- What are the fees and interest costs?

- What are the tax implications?

Pros/cons

✚ The finance is linked directly to the asset you need.

✚ It is a tax-efficient form of funding.

✚ On some leasing agreements the finance company is responsible for maintenance of the asset.

✚ It is reasonably straightforward to organize.

✚ There are lots of independent companies who are competing for your business.

Useful contacts

Use your accountant, Business Link or supplier to direct you to a local or specialist provider; **www.evp.co.uk** offers venture leasing.

	Star ratings
Ease of application	*** Fairly straightforward.
Chances of success	**** Pretty high if you have a good balance sheet and track record.
Risk level	** If you are unable to keep up repayments they will take the asset away, perhaps take you to court, and you will get a bad credit rating.
Cost	*** Reasonably low cost.
Suitability for seed	** Unlikely to need it – or be able to get it.
Suitability for start-ups	**** Suitable but difficult to get.
Suitability for early stage	***** Ideal as part of the funding mix.
Suitability for expanding businesses	***** Perfect.
Suitability for turnaround	***** Perfect for releasing some cash back into the business by refinancing existing assets.

INVOICE FINANCE COMPANIES

Again, the main banks offer invoice finance through internal divisions or associated companies, but it's generally best to find an independent provider that is more competitive.

How does it work?

Invoice finance (or 'factoring') is a complete solution under which the provider advances you up to 85 per cent of the value of the invoice, and then takes responsibility for collecting the debt. They issue statements and provide a full credit control service. When the invoice is paid they pay you the remaining value minus their fees.

Invoice discounting is a similar service except that you are still responsible for collecting the money and all the credit control work. In a 'disclosed' service it is marked on the invoice that you have a financial arrangement with the invoice discounting company, or you can opt for a confidential service in which the customer has no indication that you are financing your sales invoices.

Who's it suitable for?

For factoring you will need a turnover above £50,000 a year, while for invoice discounting you will need to have a turnover above £250,000 (although some providers may accept a lesser turnover if it can be seen that you will reach this level).

Who provides it?

A range of independent providers as well as divisions of the major banks.

What do they want?

- High-value invoices to low-risk customers.

- They prefer businesses that supply a tangible product to those that supply a service.

- They generally don't like you to be invoicing for advance payments, but this may be a better option for you than financing your invoices anyway.

- They will want to be sure you have water-tight terms and conditions of sale with your customers.

How do you get it?

Your accountant will be able to introduce you to some invoice finance companies, or you can see the list below, but you can also research providers on the internet.

When you apply you will need to provide up to date accounts, details of your customers, and state certain facts such as your average order value. The provider will run credit checks on you and your customers.

What to ask

- How do you go about chasing my customers for the money?

- What are your charges?

- What happens if a customer is particularly slow paying (say over 90 days)?

- Are there any of my customers that you won't allow me to fund invoices for?

Pros/cons

+ It can dramatically improve your cash flow.

+ It's cheaper than a bank overdraft.

+ It's quick and easy to use once you have the agreement set up.

▶

✚ The finance company will help you credit check your customers.

– If your customers don't pay within 90 days of the invoice date, you may have to pay the money you were advanced back to the finance company – check the small print! Could this be an issue for you?

– In some cases finance companies have caused friction between a company and its customers as a result of their style of chasing money.

– They might not accept every invoice for financing, so the funds you raise may be lower than expected.

Useful contacts

www.factors.org.uk – the trade association, with a list of their members.
www.cattlesif.co.uk
www.cif.co.uk
www.bibbyfinancialservices.com

Star ratings	
Ease of application	*** Reasonably straightforward.
Chances of success	**** Pretty high.
Risk level	**** Relatively risk-free.
Cost	**** Reasonably good value.
Suitability for seed stage	* Very unlikely to be available to you until you have more sales.
Suitability for start-ups	**** Very suitable but not always available.
Suitability for early stage	**** Can be very suitable if you need to improve cash flow. Generally better than an overdraft.

Suitability for expanding businesses	***** Perfect as long as you fit the criteria, and you have already tried and failed to get customers to pay earlier or in advance. Cash flow is king!
Suitability for turnaround	***** Ideal. Can free up cash from your sales ledger.

BUSINESS SUPPORT AGENCIES

Business Links (in England), Business Eye (in Wales), Invest Northern Ireland (in, you guessed it, Northern Ireland), Highlands and Islands Enterprise (in Scotland) and Business Gateway (also in Scotland) are the local business support agencies in the UK, and I always refer to them all as Business Links as a collective term.

They are tasked by the government, through the Regional Development Agencies, to provide support to small and medium-sized enterprises (SMEs).

Funding types

They adminisiter some grants and soft loans.

Their support also includes advice, training and acting as a gateway to the full range of government and European support available.

If you speak to an adviser, or browse an agency's website, you should be able to find out about the grants and other finance that may be available to you.

Who's it suitable for?

Small to medium-sized businesses employing less than 250 people. Grants are targeted to support actions that aid the economy or government policy, so you are likely to need to be taking on more staff, expanding your facilities, beginning exports or performing other key actions.

Who provides it?

The grants are mostly provided by the European Union, the UK government or your local council. They often channel these through the Regional Development Agencies, who in turn use the Business Links (that they manage) to connect businesses with the available grants.

What do they want?

- To promote economic growth or regeneration in certain geographic areas.

- To create jobs in certain geographic areas.

- To encourage investment in new technology.

- To encourage exporting.

- To encourage research and development.

- To encourage action in key areas of government/European policy.

How do you get it?

If you think you might meet the criteria, your Business Link can help you navigate the grants available and apply.

What to ask

- How long will the application process take?

- What are the realistic chances of success?

- How long is the form?

- What do we need to do in return for the grant?

Pros/cons

✚ It's money you don't have to pay back.

− It can take forever to apply for.

− There are very strict rules and criteria for assessing applications that you have to wriggle through.

− You are unlikely to be able to start the project in question until the grant has been approved.

- There is likely to be a requirement for reports to be written by you or the grant provider at intervals over the grant period, or at the end.

Useful contacts

www.businesslink.gov.uk to find your local UK business support agency.

Star ratings	
Ease of application	*** Can be a bit of a struggle to find out what is actually available in your area or industry in the first place, and then there can be quite a bit of paperwork.
Chances of success	*** Not guaranteed to say the least, because there are so many hoops to jump through for most grants, but it's worth a go.
Risk level	***** No harm in trying, and you don't have to pay the money back.
Cost	***** Very low cost.
Suitability for seed	*** There may be a few things you can tap into.
Suitability for start-ups	***** There's very likely to be some support you can access – just be prepared to work hard to find it and apply. Don't give up easily!
Suitability for early stage	**** There may well be grants to help you acquire equipment, begin e-commerce, recruit staff, etc.

Suitability for expanding businesses	**** You may be able to get grants to help with taking on and training new staff, expanding your facilities, exporting, IT, etc.
Suitability for turnaround	**** Any source of free money is worth a go!

UNIVERSITIES

If you are a student or researcher at a UK university, or if you believe your idea could be developed in partnership with a university, then it's well worth knowing that they have been given substantial funds and incentives by the government to encourage the development of businesses from research ideas, working in partnership with local companies. Your local university may well have an enterprise development manager (or someone with a similar title), who can steer you in the right direction.

Funding types

- **Equity**. The university takes a stake in your company in return for injecting capital, much of which is provided to them by the government.

- **Blagging**. They may also provide you with office/workshop/lab space to house your business, and perhaps even some time from their staff.

Who's it suitable for?

- Companies spun out from university research projects.

- Businesses with a technological or scientific opportunity.

- Businesses that require research and development expertise.

Who provides it?

Your local university, or a university that specializes in your field of expertise.

What do they want?

- To earn lots of money in the long term.

- Prestige from having been involved in a successful venture.

- Brownie points from the government.

How do you get it?

Start by speaking to a representative at your local university. There are many options, and they will be able to advise which they can offer.

What to ask

- What do you want to get out of this deal?

- What can you contribute over and above the funding?

Pros/cons

✚ Having a university as one of your shareholders will give you a lot of credibility.

✚ Depending on your opportunity the university might have useful, very expensive equipment that you otherwise couldn't afford.

✚ Easy access to a cheap workforce of students to help you.

✚ Access to research expertise.

− Some academics aren't very aware of the importance of sales compared to the joy of research.

− Some universities can be quite greedy when it comes to the amount of equity they demand in your business.

− They can move exceedingly slowly.

− They can be very risk averse.

Useful contacts

Business Link may be able to put you in touch with the right person, otherwise simply contact your local university.

Case study

Google's very first steps were taken while they were under the wing of their university. Sergey and Larry were at Stanford University in California, USA. They were postgraduates operating out of a small office in a campus building – an office that was filled with computers hosting their new search engine. As the business began to develop their professor arranged for the university to give them a $10,000 grant as seed-funding for the business, allowing them to set up the proper computer systems they needed to demonstrate their idea to potential investors.

Star ratings	
Ease of application	** Fairly straightforward.
Chances of success	**** Pretty high.
Risk level	*** Nothing too serious, but read the small print.
Cost	** Universities can be quite greedy with the amount of equity they demand. Negotiate.
Suitability for seed	***** Very suitable.
Suitability for start-ups	***** Very suitable.
Suitability for early stage	***** Very suitable.
Suitability for expanding businesses	** Unlikely to be able to raise enough money.
Suitability for turnaround	** Unlikely to be available as they are interested in new technologies, etc.

BUSINESS INCUBATORS

Incubators are sometimes affiliated to universities or business support agencies, but some are independent.

How does it work?

The incubator provides you with workspace, which can be an office or a workshop. They also provide a reception and phone answering service, and other facilities such as internet access. There may also be a loan to your business, or some form of equity investment.

Who's it suitable for?

Seed and start-up companies.

What do they want?

To earn money on the investment in you and to meet the requirements of their funding from government or other agencies, such as creating new jobs, increasing the number of new businesses or improving the survival rate of businesses.

How do you get it?

Your Business Link should be able to point you in the direction of your local incubators. You can find details at the website in 'Useful contacts' below, or simply search on the internet.

What to ask

- What services do you provide?
- Is there any limit on how long my business can be in the incubator?

- What happens as my business grows?

- What do you expect in return for providing the service in terms of fees and equity, if anything?

Pros/cons

✚ This can be a nice easy way to start, with all the facilities you need.

✚ It's good to have the moral support of other similar businesses in the incubator.

✚ Easy access to help and advice.

✚ Access to useful contacts for funding for your next stage of growth.

− They may demand to be given shares in your business – are they the kind of people you want to have shares?

Useful contacts

www.ukbi.co.uk

Star ratings	
Ease of application	***** Very easy.
Chances of success	**** Pretty high.
Risk level	**** Low risk, as long as equity isn't involved.
Cost	**** Relatively low cost, depending on what the equity requirement is.
Suitability for seed	**** Quite suitable, but may be more than you need just yet.
Suitability for start-ups	***** Very suitable.
Suitability for early stage	***** Very suitable.
Suitability for expanding businesses	* You're probably too big.
Suitability for turnaround	* You're probably too big.

OTHER BUSINESS SUPPORT

As well as Business Links and incubators there are a number of other sources for funds from government-backed agencies.

How does it work?

The agencies are given money by government, with a specific purpose to achieve. If your business fits their criteria they can provide grants, soft loans or sometimes equity investments into your company.

Who's it suitable for?

All stages of development.

Who provides it?

- **NESTA is the National Endowment for Science, Technology and the Arts.** They have a venture fund that aims to support early-stage companies that have world-class potential. They can make an initial investment of up to £150,000.

- **Community Development Venture Funds.** These support SMEs at all stages of growth, as long as they are located within the most deprived 25 per cent of the areas in England. The first such fund, Bridges Ventures, has £40m to invest in deals of between £100,000 and £2m.

- **The Local Investment Fund.** This was set up by the government in 1995 with the support of Business in the Community and the private sector. It can make loans of between £25,000 and £100,000 to social enterprises.

- **The Regional Community Loan Funds.** These were set up by the Local Investment Fund in eight regions of England. They are able to make loans of between £15,000 and £100,000 in social enterprises in their area.

- **The Adventure Capital Fund.** This can provide loans, grants and equity-type investments to social enterprises and community organizations in England.

- **Early Growth Funds.** These are regionally based government funded investment funds that provide equity funding to early-stage businesses. These can make maximum investments of up to £100,000.

- **The Community Development Finance Association.** This represents a group of organizations that has been funded by the government to provide loans or equity investment in small businesses in deprived areas.

What do they want?

To meet the objectives they have been set by government (such as creating jobs, supporting hi-tech businesses, etc.).

How do you get it?

Start by visiting the agency's website, and then approach them directly for more information. Business Links may also be able to guide you.

What to ask

- What are the criteria for your funding?

- In what ways do you provide funding?

Pros/cons

+ Access to cheap or even free money.

+ Help and advice can also be provided.

- The criteria are normally very specific and therefore most businesses won't fit in.

Useful contacts

www.nesta.org.uk – the National Endowment for Science, Technology and the Arts.

www.bridgesventures.com – the first Community Development Venture Fund.

www.lif.org.uk – The Local Investment Fund.

www.lif.org.uk/regional.htm – The Regional Community Loan Funds.

www.adventurecapitalfund.org.uk – The Adventure Capital Fund.

www.sbs.gov.uk/sbsgov/action/layer?topicId=7000000154 – the catchy, easy to remember web address of the Early Growth Funds.

www.cdfa.org.uk – The Community Development Finance Association (make sure you put the .uk on the end of you'll end up at the California Domestic Ferret Association – and I'm not kidding!)

Star ratings	
Ease of application	** There's a lot of hidden away government funding out there. It's hard to find, and there are lots of catches to do with geographic location, type of business, the type of work you do, etc. Expect lots of paperwork!
Chances of success	***High if you meet all the criteria, but there are lots of criteria!
Risk level	**** Low risk.
Cost	***** Very low cost.
Suitability for seed	**** Potentially quite suitable.
Suitability for start-ups	***** Very suitable.
Suitability for early stage	**** Potentially quite suitable.
Suitability for expanding businesses	** Unlikely.
Suitability for turnaround	** Unlikely.

CHARITIES

Some charities and trusts provide grants and soft loans to small businesses.

How does it work?

The organization can either provide a grant, or will make a soft loan (a loan with a very low interest rate) to your business. They will also provide you with advice and support, plus you get the chance to network with other entrepreneurs at their events.

Who's it suitable for?

Start-up and very early-stage businesses, particularly if the entrepreneur is under the age of 30 and has been unable to raise funding elsewhere.

Who provides it?

The Prince's Trust is the most famous, but Shell Livewire also provides support. Both organizations provide mentoring as well as the funding, which can be equally valuable in the long run.

What do they want?

- To support disadvantaged young people.

- To encourage young people to achieve their ambitions.

How do you get it?

If you meet the criteria, visit the website and ask for further information. The Prince's Trust has regional co-ordinators who can meet you and help you prepare to apply for funds or support.

What to ask

- Please?

Pros/cons

+ Free or cheap money.

+ Mentoring support.

+ Networking with other entrepreneurs.

− Restrictive in who can apply – you need to be 30 or under and unable to raise finance elsewhere.

Useful contacts

www.princes-trust.org
www.shell-livewire.org

Star ratings	
Ease of application	**** Straightforward if you meet the criteria.
Chances of success	**** Pretty high if you meet the criteria.
Risk level	***** Non-existent.
Cost	***** Free or cheap.
Suitability for seed	***** Perfect.
Suitability for start-ups	***** Very suitable.
Suitability for early stage	* Probably not eligible.
Suitability for expanding businesses	* Probably not eligible.
Suitability for turnaround	* Probably not eligible.

THE LOTTERY

Sometimes referred to as a 'stupidity tax', the lottery involves you paying money with the sure knowledge that you are likely to get back less money than you pay over the long run – but with the most miniscule of chances that you might win a lot more.

How does it work?

Millions of people pay money to play the lottery each week, many dreaming of big houses or fast cars and believing that winning millions is their only route to happiness. The lottery company pays back a fraction of this money to a fraction of the people who took part.

They do pay a proportion of the rest to 'good causes', and some people use this to justify buying the ticket – but it is much better to give the whole pound to charity if that is your reasoning.

Who's it suitable for?

People who like to lose money.

Who provides it?

Camelot currently operates the UK national lottery.

What do they want?

Your money.

How do you get the funding?

You have to pick six numbers and mark them on your entry form. Hand this to your newsagent who will feed it into the computer. Then wait for the draw with bated breath; and just so you don't get too excited, here are the odds:

- Matching all six numbers: 1 in 13,983,816.

- To win a tenner: 1 in 57.

What to ask

- Why do 57 people effectively club together to buy £10 for £57, and then agree that one of them keeps the tenner (based on the odds of winning a tenner)?

- Why do people not take responsibility for making their own dreams happen, rather than hoping (against the odds) to win a lot of money for no work?

Pros/cons

+ If you win, it's easy money.

− You won't win.

Useful contacts

Your local newsagent.

Case study

I went out and bought a lottery ticket as a research project for this book. I didn't win anything with it. Out of all the sources of funding in this book, this one is the hardest way to get any money.

Star ratings	
Ease of application	***** Very easy.
Chances of success	* Exceedingly low.
Risk level	* The most likely outcome is that it will cost you more than you earn from it.
Cost	* The most expensive tenner you've ever bought.
Suitability for seed	* Don't even think about it – you need that pound!
Suitability for start-ups	* Not at all suitable.
Suitability for early stage	* Not at all suitable.
Suitability for expanding businesses	* Go to Vegas instead to have fun with your hard-earned cash.
Suitability for turnarounds	It's no mistake that there are no stars at all here. You need that pound!

COMING SOON

The government has announced a new initiative for encouraging investment in early-stage companies, called the Enterprise Capital Funds (ECFs).

These funds will be managed either by an authorized fund manager acting on behalf of the investors in the fund, or by a group of business angels who can invest their own funds through the ECF.

Investors will be offered significant financial benefits if they invest in ECFs, probably in terms of income tax and capital gains tax incentives.

At the time of writing, the scheme has received clearance from the European Commission, and the Small Business Service is assessing bids it has received to run the programme.

I'll keep you up to date on any developments at **www.flyingstartups. com/updates**

7

CHAPTER SEVEN

Selecting a funding mix

We have now looked at all the different types of funding and the sources that you can obtain them from.

There's no shortage of money out there looking for good business-people and ideas to back, so don't just rush into getting any kind of finance (remember what I said about entrepreneurs running to their high street bank?) – spend some time to put together the right package of finance for your needs. Having a mix will reduce your reliance on any single funding source, will give reassurance to each funder and will probably reduce your overall costs of finance, as well as protecting your control of the company by ensuring that no single funder holds all the cards.

The factors to take into account when selecting a funding mix are: the stage of your business; the amount of funding you are seeking; and what is being funded.

THE STAGE OF YOUR BUSINESS

Depending on the growth stage you are at in your company, you could include the following funding sources for consideration:

- **Seed**. You, family, friends, contacts, the big banks, business support agencies, other business support, universities, business incubators, charities.

- **Start-up**. Customers, you, family, friends, contacts, suppliers, business angel networks, Regional Venture Capital Funds, the big banks, other debt funders, asset finance companies, invoice finance companies, business support agencies, other business support, universities, business incubators, charities.

- **Early stage.** Customers, you, family, friends, contacts, suppliers, business angel networks, investment exchanges, venture capital firms, Regional Venture Capital Funds, the big banks, other debt funders, asset finance companies, invoice finance companies, business support agencies, other business support, universities, business incubators.

- **Growth.** Customers, you, contacts, suppliers, business angel networks, investment exchanges, OFEX, AIM, venture capital firms, Regional Venture Capital Funds, the big banks, other debt funders, asset finance companies, invoice finance companies, business support agencies, other business support.

- **Turnaround.** Customers, you, family, friends, contacts, suppliers, business angel networks, venture capital firms, Regional Venture Capital Funds, the big banks, other debt funders, asset finance companies, invoice finance companies, business support agencies, other business support.

THE AMOUNT OF FUNDING YOU ARE SEEKING

- **Under £20k.** Customers, you, family, friends, contacts, suppliers, the big banks, other debt funders, business support agencies, other business support, universities, business incubators, charities.

- **£20k–£100k.** Customers, you, family, friends, contacts, suppliers, business angel networks, investment exchanges, the big banks, other debt funders, asset finance companies, invoice finance companies, business support agencies, other business support, universities.

- **£100k–£1m.** Customers, contacts, suppliers, business angel networks, investment exchanges, OFEX, Regional Venture Capital Funds, the big banks, other debt funders, asset finance companies, invoice finance companies, business support agencies, other business support, universities.

- **£1m+.** Customers, suppliers, business angel networks, investment exchanges, OFEX, AIM, venture capital firms, Regional Venture Capital Funds, the big banks, other debt funders, asset finance companies, invoice finance companies, business support agencies, other business support.

WHAT IS BEING FUNDED

You will have a number of reasons for raising money for your business, and your funding mix should deal with all of these, securing suitable finance for each.

- **Short-term negative cash flow.** This is more suited to invoice finance, getting early payment from your customers, delaying payment (by agreement) to your suppliers, or through an overdraft with a big bank or other debt funder.

- **Acquiring assets.** Consider asset finance, or a loan from a big bank or other debt funder. You may be able to get a grant towards some of the cost from a business support agency.

- **Creating employment.** This may well attract a grant or soft loan from a business support agency, or other business support.

- **Investing in research and development.** Universities are interested in backing this sort of project. You may be able to get grants or soft loans from business support agencies. Otherwise it's best to fund this sort of work through equity investment from contacts, business angel networks, venture capital firms or Regional Venture Capital Funds.

- **Developing a prototype product.** You may be able to get a grant from business support, otherwise this is a case for equity funding from you, friends, family, contacts or business angel networks. For big projects, venture capital firms and Regional Venture Capital Funds may be interested.

- **General start-up funding.** This is most suited to equity investment by you, friends, family or contacts. More ambitious start-ups may attract funding from business angel networks. You might decide to add a small amount of debt funding from a big bank or other debt funder. It's also worth exploring grants or soft loans from business support agencies, charities or other business support.

- **Exporting.** Grants are available from business support agencies; and invoice finance companies and big banks will be able to help too.

- **Sales and marketing.** Look for help from suppliers, customers, contacts, business angel networks, big banks, other debt funders and, if you're big enough, venture capital funds and Regional Venture Capital Funds.

Equity investment and debt finance can be used to fund most types of business activity, but the above show some different options for special cases.

APPLYING FOR FUNDING

Once you have decided on the funding mix you will aim for, you should prepare an action plan for approaching the funders and applying for finance. Put together a few notes on what you need to raise from each source.

Next do your research and find particular contacts you want to approach in each case. Who else have they funded? What can you find out about those companies? How are they doing? Can you ask them what they think of the funder? How can you get an introduction to the funder? Otherwise, how is it best to approach them? By telephone? Letter? Appointment?

In Chapter 6 I explained how to apply for each type of finance, so you should follow that guidance for each source you plan to approach.

8

CHAPTER EIGHT
Negotiating the deal

After all the work that it takes to find the right types and sources of finance for their business, many entrepreneurs are just so grateful if anybody says 'yes' that they don't realize that there is still plenty of negotiation to be done. You should know that everything is negotiable, and spend some time to reach the best possible deal. In this chapter we will look at the different negotiable terms of each type of finance.

TERMS FOR EQUITY FINANCE

Equity investors will be seasoned negotiators with a sharp business brain, so you need to prepare well and seek plenty of input from your advisers. Venture capitalists (VCs) will first negotiate a term sheet with you – which is a non-legally binding document setting out the key points of the deal. Once this is signed they will do the due diligence, and then come back to negotiate further before preparing the final documentation. Business angels and other equity investors are likely to go straight to the main negotiation.

The key points that will be negotiated by equity investors are as follows.

Valuation

This is the key part of the deal – how much your company is worth now. They will want to agree a low valuation, so they buy their shares cheaply and they have more opportunity to make a greater amount of money. You will want to negotiate a higher valuation.

The three main ways to value a business are:

1. Calculate the valuation by comparison to other similar companies.

When shares in a business are traded on a stock exchange, or a company is sold to a trade buyer, the shares are often valued on a multiple of earnings. The earnings are the annual profits of the company after tax, and the multiple tends to vary by industry, and the stage that the company is at. Let's take a rough example that BloggsCo has sold for £100m, and it's annual profits after tax are £10m. That means it has sold for an earnings multiple of 10. If you were a similar type of company, at a similar stage, you could expect to get a similar earnings multiple, so multiply your annual profits by 10 to get a rough valuation.

This rule of thumb can be affected by:

1. The company you are comparing yourself to being a quoted company whose shares are more easily tradeable, earning it a premium price.

2. If you or the comparison company is in a trend of rapid growth or decline.

3. If you or the comparison company has got a great and highly recognizable brand name.

4. If you or the comparison company has investors competing to be able to invest.

5. If you or the comparison company has valuable, and well-protected, patents, registered designs or trademarks.

6. The quality of customers that you or the comparison company has.

7. The quality of the management team at either company.

2. Calculate the valuation that gives investors their required rate of return.

If, for example, your investor requires an annual return of 20 per cent, you can take the valuation you expect to be able to achieve for the business at exit, working back to get the valuation now that will enable the return to be achieved.

To do this calculation:

1. Multiply the profit you expect to make in the year in which you plan to exit the investors by the earnings multiple (as discussed in point 1 above). For example, £2,000,000 by 10 for a small retail chain. This is the valuation that you expect the investors to exit at in the future, and we'll call this (A). In our example it equals £20,000,000.

2. Express the investor's annual rate of return as a decimal figure – so if it's 20 per cent, this would be shown as 0.2. Add 1 to this figure, giving 1.2 in this result, because it's an increase on the present position (which equals 1). We'll call this (B).

3. Multiply (B) by itself as many times as there are years between now and the planned exit. So, if this is in five years, our example would be:

$1.2 \times 1.2 \times 1.2 \times 1.2 \times 1.2 = 2.48832$ (this can also be expressed as 1.2 to the power of 7). We'll call this result (C).

4. Divide (A) by (C), giving £8,037,551 in our example as the current valuation of the company that will allow investors to make the required rate of return.

3. **Pick a figure out of thin air.**

   This isn't as daft as it sounds. Someone with good business experience will be able to come up with a pretty good valuation simply from their instincts and previous experience. It's like an estate agent deciding what price to put a house on the market for after just walking around it – someone who spent weeks working out mathematical formulae might not come up with a better valuation.

There are a range of other potential valuation methods too, but no single 'right' way. Often funders will work through each one and then come up with a figure based on all the different results.

However, a valuation figure is worthless if nobody will actually pay that amount, so the valuation will have to be open to negotiation, just as it would be if you were selling your house.

If there are other potential buyers, you can play them off against each other to get a higher valuation, or at least to avoid being negotiated down – but if there are no other buyers and you need a quick sale then you may have to accept a lower price.

Your accountants or corporate finance advisers can help you decide on the best method of valuation for your business, as it depends very much on your industry, size of company, age of business, etc.

Structure of investment

The investor will be seeking to structure their investment in your business in such a way that they are protected by having certain rights, and these rights are achieved by selecting or mixing particular classes of shares.

Ordinary shares

As the name suggests these are the standard class of share, and will typically be the class of share that you and your management team hold. Business angels will often take their investment in this class of share too, but VCs are unlikely to. These are equity shares and have votes.

'A' ordinary shares (preferred ordinary shares)

These shares bring special rights to the owner, such as being paid dividends or capital ahead of ordinary shares. The official documents of the company may specify a certain dividend that must be paid. These are equity shares and have votes. VCs may use this class of share to make their investment.

Preference shares

These shares receive dividends and capital ahead of all other classes, and usually have a defined dividend. They may also have a defined fixed date for redemption, and perhaps at a fixed premium, or they may be irredeemable. It may also be specified that they are to be convertible into either ordinary shares or 'A' ordinary shares. VCs may use this class of share to make their investment. These are non-equity shares and carry no voting rights.

Loan

In some cases VCs or angels may also provide some of their investment in the form of a secured or unsecured loan. This will be more expensive than a bank loan but rank behind the bank for payment. The terms of the loan agreement may specify that it can be converted into equity.

Directorship

In many cases your investor may want to take a seat on the board of directors, or appoint someone else to represent them. This is almost a certainty with VC investments. Don't automatically resist this, as the newcomer can often bring a wide experience, great contacts and a fresh vision that can really help the company, but do seek to agree jointly on a suitable person – you'll want someone that you can work with.

Warranties and indemnities

This is the serious bit of negotiating with VCs (it's not normally applicable in the smaller business angel deals) and an area where your lawyers and their lawyers will do battle.

The aim of warranties is for the investor to get the company *and its management team* – so you will be personally liable – to contractually promise that the information they have given the investor about the company is correct. These agreements govern to what extent you can be held accountable for the performance of the company, any legal, financial or taxation problems it encounters, and other issues that may arise.

So, for example, if they invest £1m in your company and later find out that you had heard a few weeks before signing the deal that your biggest customer was planning to change supplier (and you hadn't told them), you would be in breach of warranty.

If you breach the warranties then you will have to compensate the investor, and how this will be achieved will be set out in the indemnities.

Be sure to seek legal advice on the warranties and indemnities you are being asked to provide.

Performance agreements

VCs may seek to put in place agreements on company performance that either allow management to increase their stake if the company does particularly well, or allow the VC to increase their stake if the company doesn't meet targets. These are also known as 'ratchets'.

Approval/veto rights

The investor may require that certain decisions are referred to them for approval. This could be taking on debt over a certain amount, recruiting a new member of senior management, the issuing of new equity, etc.

Information rights

This will set out the company's obligations to provide the investor with management accounts, forecasts, budgets, annual accounts and so on.

Commitments from management and key staff

Equity investors will want to be sure that your management team are financially committed to the success of the business, so will insist on your making an investment that is sizeable for your financial position. They will also be keen to lock you and key staff into tight employment contracts with longer notice and anti-compete periods.

Anti-dilution measures

A term sheet from a VC is likely to include clauses that deal with future funding rounds and protect their position. This may be done by automatically issuing them with new shares in future rounds, particularly if the company has hit problems and the valuation is lower. There are other mechanisms too.

Tag along

If the management team receive an offer to buy their shares, then a 'tag-along' clause could require that the investor receives the same deal.

Drag along

A drag-along clause forces the hand of minority investors if a majority decides to sell the company.

Tax relief

The government runs an Enterprise Investment Scheme that offers tax relief to external investors in qualifying businesses. The requirements to qualify are fairly straightforward with most SMEs able to participate – and you won't believe how easy the paperwork is for this scheme!

The scheme offers the investors the following highly attractive benefits:

1. They can deduct a sum equal to 20 per cent of their investment in your company from their next income tax return.

2. The investor can defer gains that have been made on a different asset or investment within the last three years before investing in your company, or within one year after investing in your company.

3. If the investor holds on to their shares for at least three years then they will pay no capital gains tax when they do eventually sell the shares.

4. If the investor loses money on their investment in your business, their loss can be set against their capital gains tax or income tax bills for the year in which the loss is realized. This means that a higher rate taxpayer can claw back 40 per cent of any loss – significantly protecting the investor if the worst happens to the business.

5. After being held for more than two years, the shares the investor holds in your company are exempt from inheritance tax.

Full details can be found at **www.hmrc.gov.uk/eis/eis-index.htm**

This is an absolutely brilliant scheme, and I urge you to look into whether it could be suitable for your company. Being registered, and being able to explain the benefits to investors (friends, family, contacts and business angels), will make investing in your company very much more attractive to them. Furthermore, investors who know about it are likely to require you to register under the scheme as a condition of their investment.

The final, formal documentation

The investor will insist on having a solid shareholders' agreement in place, as well as updating the company's Memorandum and Articles of Association, and so should you. These documents will clearly set out the agreed rules for governing the company, and help avoid disputes. Where disputes do arise it will provide the method through which they will be resolved.

The memorandum and articles are the documents that were files at Companies House when your company was set up (if you have already been through the process of forming a limited company). It's likely that they were just a standard off-the-shelf set of documents then, and will need to be updated to reflect the new types of share (if applicable), voting rights and procedures, and other points agreed with your investors. These documents set out the purpose of the company and the powers granted to the directors by the company's owners (the shareholders).

The shareholders' agreement sets out the obligations that shareholders have to each other, and will include agreed terms on what would happen if a shareholder were to die, if one wanted to sell their shares, if one wanted to join the board and so on.

A note on equity versus debt

Many entrepreneurs are nervous about 'giving away control' by selling shares in their business. They either refuse to do it or refuse to award enough shares for the level of investment. You only have to watch a couple of episodes of BBC TV's *Dragons' Den* to see what I mean. Investors who buy equity in your business are taking a massive risk, because if the business doesn't work they lose all their money. It's only if you become very rich that they also make money. They share in both the upside and the downside. Debt financiers aren't interested in bearing any risk of the downside. You'll have to give security, perhaps even your home, and if there is any slight hint that things are going wrong they will seek to call in their debt without much hesitation at all – and this has sent many businesses under. So don't think you are keeping control by going for debt finance rather than equity finance.

It's also worth noting that equity financiers generally bring much more than just their money. Time and again entrepreneurs find that their business angel or VC has a fantastic contacts book and can put them in touch with some very useful people. They also have a lot of business experience and can help you avoid common pitfalls and take opportunities you would otherwise have missed.

Debt finance also saddles you with repayments and interest, which can drag down the cash flow of your company. Equity finance simply provides you with the cash, and the investors wait until the business is working and profitable before taking any cash out again.

TERMS FOR DEBT FINANCE

Debt finance is generally easier to negotiate, because the provider will be less involved in your business, and the negotiations are just about the actual deal, rather than the ongoing relationship. Most of these terms for negotiation are the same for asset finance.

Interest rate

Although this may seem set in stone to you, there is frequently room to negotiate – even with high street banks. Always try to get a lower interest rate. This will save you a lot of money in the long run.

Repayment term

This is generally negotiable too. A longer repayment term could help your cash flow, but it will make the debt more expensive.

Repayment holiday

If you're trying to improve your cash flow you may be able to negotiate a repayment holiday, during which you only pay interest. However, this does mean that the debt costs you a lot more in the end.

Early settlement penalties

Many finance providers don't like you repaying your debts early, because they earn less interest as a result, so they will often try to discourage this by including early settlement penalties in debt finance agreements.

Security

In terms of asset finance, this is easy. The security is the asset in question. When it comes to other forms of debt finance, the provider will seek security in the following ways: debenture/fixed and floating charge; personal guarantees or the Small Firms Loan Guarantee Scheme.

Debenture/fixed and floating charge

This is a legal charge over the assets in question, and often all the assets the business owns. I guarantee that your bank will ask for this if you so much as want to borrow a pound for a cup of coffee. In negotiation you should seek to limit the scope of the security and the term. If it is to secure a term loan, insist that the debenture expires when the term loan is paid off.

Personal guarantees

Again, your bank will almost certainly ask for these if your business is a limited company and you want to borrow absolutely anything at all. A recent court case means that the fixed and floating charge can no longer be considered as sufficient security for an overdraft, so if you want an overdraft the bank will want a personal guarantee.

I have always refused. I have invested substantial amounts of money and time into my companies already. If they want to make money out of me they should take some small element of risk too. There's also the principle that personal guarantees pretty much remove the purpose for having a limited company in the first place.

If you give the bank a personal guarantee and there is a problem with the business – or even if the bank gets a little worried that there might be a problem – they can demand repayment of the overdraft, and perhaps the loan too. And if the business can't repay immediately they can come after you personally, including your home.

Be ultra-wary of personal guarantees. If you are thinking about agreeing to one be sure to talk it over with your partner first, and perhaps also an accountant or other adviser.

Guarantee

In some circumstances you can get someone to guarantee a loan for you. Some parents have done this with small amounts to help their children start up in business. If you own other companies, you can arrange for a more established company to guarantee the loan of a newer business.

Sometimes business angels will offer to guarantee a loan as part of their investment. It's efficient for them as, unless things go wrong, they don't actually have to pay over any money and can invest it elsewhere. Make sure you look out for their interests too, and ensure that the guarantee is linked only to that loan and is for a fixed period.

Small Firms Loan Guarantee Scheme

If you can't provide enough security through other means then the government can help. The Small Firms Loan Guarantee Scheme is provided through the major banks, and means that the government will guarantee 75 per cent of the loan amount, which can be for up to £250,000 and for a term of up to ten years.

Businesses of most types which are less than five years old, with a turnover of under £5.6m, are eligible.

In return for this guarantee, you pay the Department for Trade and Industry a premium of 2 per cent of the outstanding balance.

These arrangements changed on 1 December 2005, so don't get confused if you see out-of-date information on this scheme.

In all your negotiations you should be polite but firm. Don't be shy to stick up for yourself and what you think is fair. And you wouldn't be an entrepreneur if you didn't try to get a better deal in some way.

The key, however, is to be professional. It has been known for entrepreneurs to shout, stomp around or even walk out of key negotiations, and that's not going to get you a better deal – it's more likely to prompt the funders to walk away.

9

CHAPTER NINE
After raising the funding

You have put so much effort into raising the funding for your business that it would be a shame to fritter it away.

Raising finance is only the start of managing the funding of your business – it's a continuous process that doesn't stop when an investor's cheque hits your bank account.

It's now more important than ever that you maintain tight financial controls in your business, and that you really use every single penny to its maximum potential.

CELEBRATE

There is never enough celebration in business. You've achieved something fantastic in raising the funding you need – celebrate! Involve everyone and get them excited about the future, and the fact that experienced outside funders believe in what you all do and are excited about your future as well.

MAKE SURE EVERYBODY KNOWS WHAT THEY ARE SUPPOSED TO BE DOING

In your business plan you committed to achieving certain things. You set out critical success factors and an action plan. You also put together detailed financial forecasts.

As the entrepreneur, it's your job to show everyone the direction that the business is going in and what is required of them to get there, and to encourage them to feel committed and excited about it.

Be clear, be demanding, be inspiring.

MANAGE THE CASH FLOW

Just because you suddenly have a lot of money, it does not mean you can go out on an expensive spending spree, or not worry so much about finding new customers. If you're not careful with the cash, you may find yourself back on the funding trail in a year's time – but this time with a dented reputation.

Make sales and collect the money

The most important thing now is to work very hard to deliver, or beat, the sales forecasts in your plan. Get started straight away. Put together the sales materials you need, find target customers and start selling. Put in place credit control procedures so that you get paid, and get paid on time, by your customers.

Manage expenditure

If they are not there already, put in place tight budgets for expenditure, and controls to monitor it. Expenditure above a certain amount should require approval from the management team, and really high expenditure should require the approval of two directors at least.

Tighten up the other financial systems, so that managers have to sign off the expenses claims of staff – and even your expenses should be approved and signed off by someone else.

Always shop around to get the things you need at the best value (which isn't always cheapest – you may pay a bit more for something that is higher quality, or lasts longer, etc.).

Don't forget your blagging skills!

And most of all – don't go out and buy/lease a flashy car! The one you have will be fine for another year or two. Fund flashiness out of profits only.

Weekly cash flow forecast

As part of your new-found tightness with cash, you and the rest of the management team should study a weekly cash flow forecast.

Prepare it to show the next three months broken down week by week, and as each week goes by add another week to the end of the forecast so you can always see three months ahead.

You should have a formal weekly meeting in which you look at this forecast and:

1. **Make note of the important things that have to happen in order to stick to it.** Get the people concerned to commit to making them happen. You must be honest if you think a payment from a customer might be delayed, or if something else on the forecast may not be quite right. This is an internal forecast and should be made on a worst-case scenario.

2. **Make plans to iron out any problems.** Ask a customer to pay early for a discount, ask suppliers for a couple more weeks to pay, arrange an overdraft, delay taking your salary and so on.

MEASURE AGAINST THE PLAN

Each month you should prepare management accounts showing how you performed against the business plan. Again, you and the management team should have a meeting to assess what changed for better or worse, how that impacts on the business, what needs to be done about it and whether there may be a bigger issue underlying the change.

Again, be open and honest with yourselves – don't go sticking your head in the sand. If there's a problem, face up to it straight away before it becomes a nightmare.

MANAGE THE RELATIONSHIP WITH YOUR FUNDERS

Now that they have given you their money, don't forget about your funders. It really is worth spending some time every month, or at least every quarter, to write a brief update for them on what is happening in the business.

If there's any bad news, let them know straight away, rather than trying to hide it from them. They may well be able to help or advise you, and they will have a much better opinion of you if you are open about problems. At the least they'll expect to be sent quarterly management accounts and the annual accounts. Some funders may also require to see more detailed information; this will have been specified in the agreement with you.

Your funders are also very likely to have excellent business experience and contact networks, which you can tap into if you have built a good relationship with them.

BUILD AN AMAZING BUSINESS

You've done a great job in getting this far, but this is just the beginning for you and your company. Great and exciting things lie ahead – go and use this opportunity, this springboard, to be the best in the world at whatever it is you do. Build a really amazing business.

The end

I hope you've found this book useful in your fundraising journey. I have tried to make the subject of finance more accessible to entrepreneurs like myself, and I'll be pleased if you think I've succeeded.

Although we are at the end of the book, we don't have to say 'goodbye' as I'd like to invite you to an online community I run for entrepreneurs.

WWW.FLYINGSTARTUPS.COM

This website supports all of my books and contains useful documents, contacts and other information connected to them. It's also a community of like-minded entrepreneurs who seek help, and to help each other. Many of the entrepreneurs keep online diaries there (Pilots' Logs), so you can read about the progress of other people like you.

I'm often on the site answering questions and reading the Pilots' Logs (entrepreneurs diaries) and forums, so I look forward to meeting you.

Thanks for reading, and I wish you success in your business.

Steve Parks

> **Stop Press**. In the time between writing *How to Fund Your Business* and it going to press, I've used it to work with an early-stage company that was raising £1.5m. We followed everything in this book and it worked. Phew.

how to fund
your business

PEARSON
Prentice Hall
BUSINESS

Books that make you better

Books that make you better. That make you *be* better, *do* better, *feel* better. Whether you want to upgrade your personal skills or change your job, whether you want to improve your managerial style, become a more powerful communicator, or be stimulated and inspired as you work.

Prentice Hall Business is leading the field with a new breed of skills, careers and development books. Books that are a cut above the mainstream – in topic, content and delivery – with an edge and verve that will make you better, with less effort.

Books that are as sharp and smart as you are.

Prentice Hall Business.
We work harder – so you don't have to.

For more details on products, and to contact us, visit
www.pearsoned.co.uk

Steve Parks

how to fund your business

The Essential Guide to Raising Finance to Start and Grow Your Business

PEARSON

Prentice Hall

BUSINESS

Harlow, England • London • New York • Boston • San Francisco • Toronto
Sydney • Tokyo • Singapore • Hong Kong • Seoul • Taipei • New Delhi
Cape Town • Madrid • Mexico City • Amsterdam • Munich • Paris • Milan

PEARSON EDUCATION LIMITED

Edinburgh Gate
Harlow CM20 2JE
Tel: +44 (0)1279 623623
Fax: +44 (0)1279 431059
Website: www.pearsoned.co.uk

First published in Great Britain in 2006

ISBN-13: 978-0-273-70624-3
ISBN-10: 0-273-70624-1

British Library Cataloguing-in-Publication Data
A catalogue record for this book is available from the British Library

Library of Congress Cataloging-in-Publication Data
A catalog record for this book is available from the Library of Congress

10 9 8 7 6 5 4 3 2 1
10 09 08 07 06

Typeset in 11pt Minion by 70
Printed and bound in Great Britain by Bell & Bain Ltd, Glasgow

The publisher's policy is to use paper manufactured from sustainable forests.